THE LEGISLATIVE COUNCIL

IN

THE AMERICAN STATES

THE LEGISLATIVE COUNCIL
IN THE AMERICAN STATES

William J. Siffin
Department of Government
Indiana University

Indiana University Press
Bloomington   1959

Indiana University Publications: Social Science
Series No. 18—Indiana University, Bloomington

Publication Committee
Byrum E. Carter   Albert K. Cohen

The Indiana University Publications Social Science Series was founded in 1939 for the publication of occasional papers and monographs by members of the faculty.

This book was composed at the Research Center in Anthropology, Folklore, and Linguistics.

FOREWORD

As the fund of knowledge increases, the task of selecting relevant bits of it to guide choices of action becomes increasingly complex. Once the task of the American state legislature consisted chiefly of maintaining a
rather simple consensus — of balancing, reconciling,
compromising wants. There was a body of knowledge
concerned with interpersonal relations accumulated
through many centuries of pragmatic living in the Judaic-
Christian tradition. There was also another body of
knowledge born of a few centuries of struggle against
arbitrary power. These two profound bodies of social
philosophy had become a part of the conventional wisdom of the era of the first American state legislatures—
so much so that a man chosen by his neighbors and
friends to represent them at the state capital was likely
to have a sufficient visceral comprehension of these
values to keep his votes usually within their vague limits
in dealing with the limited issues and problems of the
time.

The task of the legislature yet remains to arrive at
a consensus, to balance, reconcile, compromise wants.
But a knowledge of the Ten Commandments and due process is hardly a sufficient stock of specialized knowledge
to equip the present-day legislator to deal with all issues. The accumulation of physical and social needs
and knowledge is so great that he is not only not likely
to know enough to guide him, he cannot know enough to
guide him. He must find some way for the specialists
to pick out the relevant bits for his use.

The American state legislator's plight is not unique,
but common to every man in contemporary society.

v

How many more of my wants could I satisfy if I could know all the relevant information each time I make a decision. And with the march of knowledge the task becomes proportionately greater. The tendency is for more and more persons to become specialists while all remain laymen outside their own specialties. A fundamental problem of our time, common throughout the whole society, is just this: how to bring relevant information under the command of the decision maker, to bridge the chasm between the layman and the expert.

Professor Siffin set himself the task of observing, analyzing and evaluating the council as an instrument for bringing into focus relevant information for the legislator and the legislature. He has had the advantage of experience in the daily grind of assembling data and preparing them for the Kentucky legislature. He subsequently applied the techniques used in the service of the Kentucky Council to study the council movement itself. He pondered what he found.

He has opened the door to the study of the process of informing the legislature, and he has demonstrated the quality of the light he can throw on this pressing problem. It remains for him to explore the whole process, the formal devices which legislatures use, such as interim commissions, committees, hearings; the extra legislative devices and procedures, party organization, private representation, both formally organized and individual spontaneous petitions of the people for the redress of grievance, as the Fathers put it in the First Amendment. Perhaps his feel for private representation will be sharpened by his tour of duty in Thailand where there is none, no mechanics for its use, and little appreciation of its value. He has shown a nice instinct for singling out the factors in a situation, and a delicate sense of balance in measuring the weight of each, the momentum and inertia of institution and

custom, the drive of partisan interest, the force of personality. Fortunate indeed will it be for the legislatures
and for society if he will devote his talents to assessing
the whole range of devices and procedures for bringing
together the hard facts so that the legislator can make
an informed judgment.

December 17, 1958   John E. Stoner
Bangkok

PREFACE

The size of this volume is but a poor index of its author's debts. If these were listed in full, its length would be measurably increased.

Professor John M. Gaus more than upheld his well-earned reputation for wisdom, patience, and generosity in commenting on a draft of this study, and in again reviewing a revised version thereof. He also contributed a significant bit of the data, having served as secretary of the Wisconsin Executive Council, a forerunner of the legislative councils. However, just as his exploits in Wisconsin were not particularly intended to furnish data for this study, neither does this acknowledgement of his many kindnesses imply that he is responsible for what you find on the following pages.

To Professor John Stoner of the Indiana University Department of Government I am also deeply obligated, for painstaking review of the manuscript, for discerning suggestions, and above all else for encouragement—and occasional prodding.

Professor V. O. Key's stimulating studies of American state politics have been a considerable boon to me. I am indebted to his publisher for permission to quote a number of passages from his valuable book, American State Politics: An Introduction (Knopf, 1956).

Dr. Frederick Guild, Dr. Jack Isakoff, Dr. Jack W. Rodgers, and Messrs, M. G. Toepel, Earl Sachse, John A. Skipton, and Louis C. Dorweiler—these are among the men who have helped develop America's array of state legislative policy staff services, and to give it the substance it has today. They have also given me much of their time, and the benefits of their rich experience.

Others also contributed much in the course of interviews, including Sam Wilson of Topeka, Kansas, Professor Emeritus John P. Senning, my own former Professor Lloyd M. Short, and Professor Harold M. Davey. My obligations to these men are suggested by many of the notes which follow.

To Dr. Arthur Y. Lloyd of the Kentucky Legislative Research Commission I am indebted for memorable and stimulating lessons in the arts of politics and administration, Kentucky style, as well as for an introduction to the legislative staff agencies. Mr. Herbert Wiltse, representative par excellence of the Council of State Governments, not only gave me quite a lot of assistance, he helped me appreciate the true role of his organization— to which I am also obligated for frequent recourse to its most useful publications.

I also wish to acknowledge permission to quote at some length from the following sources: W. Brooke Graves, American State Government, 4th edition, Boston: D. C. Heath & Co., 1953; Samuel K. Gove and Gilbert Y. Steiner's discerning study of The Illinois Legislative Process, Urbana, Institute of Government and Public Affairs, University of Illinois, 1954; and from the valuable report, The Forty-eight States: Their Tasks as Policy Makers and Administrators, New York, The American Assembly, Columbia University, 1955, including particularly Karl A. Bosworth's excellent essay, "Law Making in State Governments."

As for Professor T. V. Smith's inimitable description of his role in the establishment of the Illinois Legislative Council—I have quoted in extensio from the copy of a speech which he kindly supplied; to paraphrase would have been to lose both the spirit of the venture and of the man.

I am grateful to two of my colleagues, professors Lynn Turner and Albert Cohen, who read the manuscript

and made comments both frank and helpful; and to the
Indiana University Research Foundation for a small
grant which helped finance some of my field work.

Finally—and certainly not in order of importance—
I am indebted beyond ability to ever repay my wife for
patience, encouragement, assistance, and abnegation.
She has shared in all the grief—and only some of the
fun—involved in this little study.

Wm. J. Siffin

CONTENTS

81997

TABLES

CHAPTER I

INTRODUCTION

> There is in State Legislators (particularly
> in the West) a restlessness which, coupled with
> their limited range of knowledge and undue ap-
> preciation of material interests, makes them
> rather dangerous. Meeting for only a few
> weeks in the year, or perhaps in two years,
> they are alarmingly active during those weeks,
> and run measures through whose results are
> not apprehended till months afterwards...the
> meeting of the legislature is looked forward to
> with anxiety by the "good citizens" in these
> communities, and its departure hailed as a
> deliverance.[1]

There is timelessness in Bryce's observations about
the American state legislatures. What he saw of them in
the 1880's could have been seen decades earlier— or
later. They have been objects of concern, ridicule, dis-
gust and alarm for a long time. Their weaknesses have
stimulated the imaginations of untold numbers of reformers from Benjamin Franklin to Belle Zeller. Yet
they have managed to remain vital arenas in which political forces have struggled through to momentarily adequate resolution.

The American state legislatures are curious mix-
tures of change and stability. One is tempted to describe
them as 18th Century institutions in a 20th Century setting.
Many of their contemporary characteristics stem directly
from colonial times. In popular thought they are regarded
in much the same light as in the mid-18th Century—as
controllers of the purse, determiners of policy, inhibitors

1

of a grasping executive, resolvers of political conflict,
and generally as the key instruments of self-government.[2]

But many things have changed, appearances of con-
stancy notwithstanding, and today's state legislatures are
different from those of the past. Their settings differ.
Their problems are different. We understand them dif-
ferently. They are different because of certain deliberate and sometimes significant changes in their processes.

One of these changes has been the establishment of
a device known as the "legislative council," which is
highly regarded as a contribution to the improvement of
American state legislative operations.[3]

Legislative councils have existed for almost a quarter of a century. This study seeks to assess their importance as adjuncts of our state legislatures, and to
delineate the circumstances or conditions which appear
to affect their operations and results.

The councils have been received with considerable
enthusiasm. Their spread across the states might
serve as testimony to their value. By 1958, about twenty-
five years after their inception, councils or "council-
type agencies" were to be found in 36 States.[4]   In the aggregate, they appeared to be spending about $2,500,000
a year on research and related services for state legislatures and state governments.[5]   A term, "the council
movement," had come to symbolize both the spread of
the council idea and the enthusiasm of its supporters.[6]

But enthusiasm and spectacular growth are alone no
basis for assessment. In the face of over a hundred and
fifty years of unregenerate legislating one hesitates to
ascribe revolutionary consequences to a single device,
no matter how widespread its popularity.

A critical evaluation must deal with these questions:
What is the role of the legislative council? To what extent and in what way does the council fulfil it? Does this
role make sense—or, more precisely, how significant

is it in the context of evident problems and needs affecting our contemporary legislatures? And what is the relation of the council to other types of legislative policy
staff?

The councils must be evaluated in terms of their effect upon the process of policy-making in the state legislature. Their raison d'etre is to improve the quality of
the product of our legislative assemblies, not in a pro-
cedural manner so much as in terms of the actual content
of legislative decisions.[7]

Such an assessment is not simple, nor is it likely to
be precise. Circumstances hardly permit controlled ex-
perimental observation. But a combination of approaches
gives, in the aggregate, a reasonably adequate basis for
appraising the effect which a legislative council can and
does have upon the quality of legislative decision-making.

The significance of the legislative council derives
from the nature and significance of the legislative process. This study includes certain general assumptions
about that process. They are set forth at appropriate
places.

Finally, as the councils and the legislatures and the
states themselves do not exist in isolation, an evaluation
of the councils must take some account of the broad range
of problems affecting the legislatures and the legislative
process in the states, including consequences of changing
economic, social and political settings. These are the
sources of important issues which must be faced in the
legislatures, and of questions about the continued validity
of our present pattern of governmental organization with
its great dependence upon the states and their legislatures.

Notes

1. James Bryce, The American Commonwealth
(New York: MacMillan and Co., 1891), p. 521.

2. Clinton Rossiter, The First American Revolution, Part I, Seedtime of the Republic (New York: Harcourt, Brace and Co., 1953), pp. 116-19.

3. See, for example, Belle Zeller (ed.), American
State Legislatures, Report of the Committee on American Legislatures, American Political Science Association (New York: Thomas Y. Crowell Co., 1954), pp. 124-
25.

4. The Book of the States 1958-59 (Chicago: The
Council of State Governments, 1958), pp. 60-69, 70-71.

5. Ibid.

6. See, for instance, W. Brooke Graves, American
State Government (4th ed.; Boston: D.C. Heath and Co.,
1953), p. 258.

7. The discussion in Graves, pp. 257-62, supports
the point.

CHAPTER II

THE DECLINE OF THE LEGISLATURES

The idea of political representation was accepted
and applied from the very beginnings of the American
colonial era.[1]

From 1619, when "a representative assembly broke
out in Virginia" to "The Golden Age" of the latter 18th
Century, the legislatures were molded by a fortuitous
combination of practical experience, political needs
and political ideas.

By the time of the adoption of the Constitution of
1787 the major structural characteristics and formal
concepts of the American state legislature had largely
been evolved, applied and accepted.[2]

> The most important civil factors in Ameri-
> ca at the close of the seventeenth Century . . .
> were the assemblies, elected by the qualified
> voters of the several provinces. But another
> element of great significance was the three-
> fold division of government, which though by
> no means nicely defined, was yet clear enough
> for all practical purposes, in the legislature
> chosen by the people, in the executive ap-
> pointed . . . and in the judiciary, appointed
> usually, with the assent of the council, by
> the executive.[3]

The greatest significance of this development lay
not in the particular forms, but in their lasting rele-
vance. The systems which had developed over long
years were both stable and practical. In the decades
ahead they would demonstrate their impressive viability.
The concerns of government and the character of politics

5

were to change mightily, but the essential forms of our state governments would not be radically altered or replaced. In fact, the formal similarities between the structures of state government today and those of more than a century and a half ago are deceptive; they tend to mask enormous substantive changes. And the formal system is so well established that proposals for basic modifications have never received much popular support.

The legislatures of the late 18th Century were surprisingly similar to today's in many ways, and the lines of their future development were already well established.

1. "Quite as consciously as Parliament, the several colonial legislatures rested on the principle of property rights."[4] The later ideas of direct democracy and universal suffrage were hardly applicable. Yet their seeds had been sown; institutions adaptable to democratization had been created; and a foundation for broad public representation had been laid in the vigorous thought of such men as Thomas Hooker, John Wise and later in the spirit epitomized by that professional rebel and agitator, Samuel Adams.[5]

2. During the seventeenth and eighteenth centuries, with the growth of the colonies, the practice of extending representation in colonial assemblies to new towns or counties more or less on a district or geographical basis became well established—to the point where in some cases the assemblies became unwieldy and efforts to expand them were checked by the British Board of Trade.[6]

> By easy logic a geographical theory had emerged, by the terms of which a legislator must be a freeman of the district rather than of the realm, that he should hold power for a short period and frequently submit his conduct to the scrutiny of the electors, and that a district should bear a just per capita relation to the total population.[7]

3. Despite the power of the colonial governor and his council, and of the Crown, something akin to ministerial government had developed, largely as a result of the power of the assemblies over appropriations. The Legislatures designated officials in money bills, denied the councils the right to amend appropriation legislation, and generally usurped much of the power of the executive.[8]

4. Out of the widening breach separating the colonial governor and his council from the assembly grew the bicameral structure of the legislative bodies. By 1787 all save two states had bicameral assemblies.[9] This pattern, once established, was not modified until the adoption of Nebraska's unicameral structure in 1937.

5. The prototype of a committee system developed during colonial times, to be elaborated considerably during the Revolution. Between 1776 and 1790 the standing committee really came into extensive use, to deal with numerous petitions and to clear up large amounts of legislative work resulting from the war.

By 1790 the standing committees were "the most conspicuous feature of the organization of nearly all the American assemblies," and by 1790, too, the perennial tendency for committee members to shirk their obligations was already evident.[10]

6. Other major elements of legislative procedure had been established, including the fiction of the "committee of the whole house," the use of investigative powers by committees, the legislative officers one finds today—clerk, speaker, sergeant-at-arms, and door keepers—and a standard procedure for passing bills.[11]

7. It has been asserted, too, that a practical foundation had been established for the future process of judicial review, and particularly for passage by the U.S. Supreme Court upon the constitutionality of state laws, as a

result of the colonial arrangement requiring British approval of colonial legislative enactments.[12]

8. At least a basis for future political organization
and control of the legislature had been established in the
processes of the legislatures and in the cleavage of economic interests between established propertied groups
and the underrepresented western farmers and frontiers-
men and the unrepresented workers.

> Those rebelling farmers of 1786 in Massachu-
> setts and others like them in similar economic
> circumstances were ultimately to become Jef-
> fersonian Republicans. The 'Boston interests'
> and groups with similar economic stakes later
> became the heart of the Federalist combination.[13]

The revolutionary period was actually marked by a
decline in the type of "party" activity which characterized
the colonial junta. The constitutions of the era took no
cognizance of the idea of party—despite the fact that
proto-party organizations had dominated colonial government. The wartime need for the expeditious transaction
of large volumes of business largely replaced an earlier
dominant concern with controversy with the colonial governor, and during the Revolutionary period there was but
one party.[14]

9. Finally, the legislature was viewed as the key institution ("The supreme power in every commonwealth")
in a political framework based upon Lockean ideas of
limited government, a fundamental law of nature and a
written constitution, a judiciary independent of the legislature, and at least an acknowledgment of the idea of majority rule. The object of government and legislation was
to be the public good of society— "the peace, safety and
public good of the people"— and the role of government
and law was to be the maintenance of a framework of order
for the community rather than the dominant force within
it.[15]

The legislatures and the idea of legislative supremacy
reached their apogee in the brief period between the Revolution and the turn of the 19th Century. In 1781 "the legislatures held the first place in the public esteem"; the
legislature was the nucleus of the government.[16] The
scope of legislative power was broad, limited in only two
states (Massachusetts and New York) by the executive
veto.[17] The governor was most thoroughly restrained by
constitutional provisions making him a "creature of the
legislature," and a victim of "the anti-executive feeling
of the Revolution [which] expressed itself extravagantly
in the first state constitutions."[18]

The 19th Century was marked by significant developments in the operations and powers of the state legislatures. Suffrage was broadened and patterns of representation were modified in the direction of greater equality.
The rise of the parties revolutionized legislative operations. And the legislatures soon began the long downward
drift from supremacy into a position of eclipse marked by
increasing public distrust, a multiplication of constitutional restrictions, a continuing reduction of legislative
control over the judicial branch of government, and the
gradual ascendency of the executive.[19]

"In 1789 the States were the creators of the Federal
Government; in 1861 the Federal Government was the
creator of a large majority of the States."[20] Much had
happened to the states between these years, including the
movements for internal improvements, protective tariffs,
expansionist land policies, and the like.

The frontier aura which was so significant an aspect of our politics and our society in these times worked
a complex set of consequences upon the states and their
legislatures. The frontier was in part a nationalizing
force, a movement both toward sectionalism and an ultimate overriding national unity. The needs and perspec-
tives of the frontier contributed to the elevation of the

national government, and to the gradual shifting of the
focus of our politics to issues which transcended the individual states. At the same time, an effect of the frontier was to deepen and broaden the scope of all government, as the pioneer quickly came to look to it as a
varied instrument of society. "The individualism of the
Kentucky pioneer of 1796 was giving way to the Populism
of the Kansas pioneer of 1896."[21]   This helped expand
the scope of the concerns of the state legislatures.

The democratic orientation of the frontier combined a fierce love of liberty with a pragmatic approach
to the use of government and an implicit "compact theory"
about its character. The government to which the settler
looked increasingly for service—for the state university, for example and for social control—must still remain a government of his peers. The legislators must
be men like himself, in close contact with their constituents. And if common men at times failed their trust in
the face of uncommon pressures and the requirements of
an increasingly complicated society, then they should be
circumscribed to help them remain honest representatives of a polity dedicated to freedom and the common
man.

Almost the whole theme of the first hundred years
of change in state constitutions is one of the growth of
constitutional protections against the legislature: the
executive veto, the lengthening of the governor's term of
office, the substitution of popular election for legislative
appointment of officials ("The feeling seems to be, not
that the people can choose more wisely than the legislature, but that they will choose more honestly."[22]),
limitations upon the legislature's power to borrow money,
constitutional prescription of details of legislative procedure, prohibitions against special legislation, and a
marked trend toward biennial instead of annual legislative sessions ("to lessen legislation, by taking away half
its opportunities"[23]).

The thirty-seven state constitutions adopted during
the period 1864-1879 are good—if not very vivid—docu-
mentation of the fall in popularity of the legislatures.[24]
The trend of constitutional development is illustrated by
Kentucky and the high contrast between its earliest constitutions (1792 and 1799) and that of 1890.[25] The 1799
constitution vested the legislative power in the two
branches of the General Assembly, defined the structure
of the legislature, and established limitations in the form
of a bill of rights and a prohibition against the emancipa-
tion of slaves. The 1890 constitution, containing almost
17,000 words, enumerated 29 specific subjects on which
special legislation was forbidden, limited regular sessions to 60 days per biennium, established an independent
Railroad Commission to replace legislative efforts at
transportation regulation, and in 28 detailed sections sup-
planted practically all prior legislative provisions for
the regulation of corporations. Legislative procedure
and the scope of legislative power were defined in great
detail, and the General Assembly was explicitly forbidden
ever to incur indebtedness beyond the amount of
$ 500,000.[26]
Why all these restrictions? The earlier constitutions had granted the legislature almost unlimited power
to enact special legislation, and the power had been ex-
tensively used and abused. By 1890 more than
$ 232,000,000 worth of corporation property in the com-
monwealth was untaxed because of legislative recognition
that it was "devoted to a public purpose." Many Ken-
tuckians felt that the corporations had taken over the
state. It was asserted that:

> "we have three Houses in the legislative depart-
> ment—the Senate, the House of Representatives,
> and the Third House, and that illegitimate mon-
> ster unknown to the Constitution of our fathers
> is the most potent of the three.[27]

Most of the delegates to the 1890 constitutional convention felt that the real root of Kentucky's governmental problems was the almost unlimited power of the General Assembly. One of them said that "the principal, if not the sole, purpose of the Constitution which we are here to frame, is to restrain its [the Legislature's] will and restrict its authority."[28] And in Kentucky, as elsewhere, this is exactly what was done. The legislatures were the victims of the times, first victimized by the consequences of "an ambitious industrialism that was quite cynically buying and selling the political state,"[29] and secondly by the lack of any general understanding of what was happening in America.

The finest elements of the post-Civil war reform movement are symbolized adequately by George William Curtis, "child of Puritan conscience," "idealist," political critic and leader in reform.[30] No discerning student of systems of government, Curtis placed his faith in morality; "in his anxious concern for 'good government' he failed to probe deeply the sources of 'bad government.' In the presence of the vast corruptions of the Guilded Age he was . . . helpless in diagnosing the evil. . . ."[31] Essentially, his thesis was the destruction of corrupt political machinery through civil service reform and independent voting.[32]

The naiveté reflected in the response of American political thought to the impact of economic revolution upon the legislatures is retrospectively somewhat appalling. "Every schoolboy knew that the Standard Oil had refined everything in Pennsylvania but the legislature."[33] While constitution makers were plugging some of the countless holes in the legislative structure, such pundits as E. L. Godkin were observing that

> we should probably, in a college-graduate government, witness the disappearance from legislation of nearly all acts and resolutions which are

> passed for what is called 'politics'; that is,
> for the purpose of pleasing certain bodies of
> voters, without any reference to their real
> value as contributions to the work of govern-
> ment.[34]

Some of the earliest essays in American pragmatism were written not by Ostrogorski, Lowell, Ford and
their followers, but by the 19th Century reframers of
state constitutions, who with all their myopia and false
perspective were at least working on the implicit assumption that dynamic political realities required tangible action.[35]

The consequences for the legislatures were
neither fully fortunate nor singularly effective. They
did tend to mitigate some of the worst legislative evils;
but, as state-level approaches to problems which by the
late 19th Century far transcended state boundaries,
many of the restrictive constitutional enactments were
well on the way to obsolescence by the time of their
adoption. They were documentary testimony to public
distrust of its legislative assemblies. This ham-string-
ing approach was probably as much as could be expected
in an age before the birth of modern insights into the
nature of our political processes. It was a time when
the Georgia constitution could declare lobbying to be a
crime,[36] and only a James Bryce could follow his in-
cisive, sparkling chapters on American state government with the poignant observation that the political
parties— "the steam that drives the engine"—were singularly unoriented toward the affairs of the states, while

> what the legislatures of the worst states show
> is not merely a need for the existence of a
> sound opinion, . . . but the need for methods by
> which it can be brought into efficient action up-
> on representatives. . . .[37]

In one sense, legislative institutional development
was substantially complete soon after the end of the
colonial era. In another, it was to be revolutionized by
19th Century political, social, and economic developments. The rise of the parties, the impact of the frontier, and the expanding significance of the politics of
economic interests changed the content of the legislative
process. The imposition of positive social responsibilities upon government shifted the very objectives of
political processes. The growth of a nation and national
political issues tended to subordinate the states and
their legislatures, leaving them with relatively little in
the nature of an issue-oriented politics supported by
continued and widespread public interest.

In the early 1830's, de Tocqueville could write
that "patriotism . . . is still directed to the state and has
not passed over to the Union."[38] But time disproved his
prediction that the Federal government might wither,
and the public's "more decided attachment to their separate governments in the states" was fading as he wrote.[39]

At the state level, the tyranny of the majority which
so greatly concerned de Tocqueville was never really
realized; instead, another kind of tyranny arose—the
corrosive rule of the railroads and other economic interests. De Tocqueville had written: "Of all political
institutions, the legislature is the one that is most easily
swayed. . . ."[40] And so it proved to be, but the swaying
was not the force of an irresistible majoritarianism;
it was the push of interest-dominated politics.

It took a long time to supplant an undiscerning
faith in institutional expressions of mechanical natural
laws needing only virtuous application. By then the
major focus of our politics had moved beyond the states,
and the state legislatures had lost the irresistible
powers that de Tocqueville had found in them and were
but sorry institutions, necessary evils, bound, tethered

and distrusted. As Reinsch pointed out, while the limiting of the legislatures had eliminated some evils, "a
complete solution of legislative difficulties will not be
looked for in this direction."[41] Crude attempts to lessen
the amount of legislating in the face of mounting needs
for positive governmental action were worse than fruit-
less. They did not stem the flooding tide of legislation.[42]

They did impede legislative performance and the
general functioning of governments at the very time
when effectiveness was growing more important. As
Herbert Croly later observed,

> . . . .the general work of state political re-
> organization which was carried on during the
> first century of our national life has been des-
> cribed as that of imposing increasing limita-
> tions upon the powers of the state legislatures.
> This formula emphasizes the most conspicuous
> aspect of the process, but does not define its
> essential nature. Essentially the process con-
> sisted of imposing every possible check on any
> and every positive function of state government
> . . . The result was a system of government
> which was so completely checked that it lost
> all balance.[43]

The legislatures, "not considered competent to
govern themselves" were nonetheless regarded constitutionally as "fully competent to govern most exactly
and completely the behavior of the executive. . . ."[44]
This was government by paralysis, or nearly so. In the
divergent lines of movement in 19th Century state government—toward mounting limitations in the face of
growing demands—loomed an impasse.

But changes in substance and to some extent in
form were in the offing. By the end of the 19th Century
gubernatorial leadership of the legislatures was beginning to emerge. This incipient movement was marked
by such things as the executive veto, which spread from

two states in 1788 to all but one by the early years of the
20th Century,[45] and by the spasmodic appearance of
politically strong governors in various states.

A movement for governmental reorganization was
also gathering force. It was motivated by concern with
economy and efficiency, symbolized to a considerable extent by the rallying cry of "the short ballot," and focused
upon the integration and rationalization of the administrative structure and executive leadership of state governments.[46] The merit system, executive budget, and
non-partisan elections were among its features. It was
something of a synthesis of 19th Century idealism and
20th Century pragmatism.[47]

The legislatures were inevitably affected by these
developments. Governors became legislative leaders
as a result of such devices as the executive budget and
more focused patterns of state politics which made some
of them powerful political leaders.[48] The growing size
and complexity of the executive branches of state governments increased their power vis-a-vis the legislatures.
Yet during this latter-day period of reform which began with the comprehensive Illinois reorganization of
1917 no basic revisions were made in the essential structures of the legislatures, except in Nebraska.[49]

Inside many state legislatures, some changes in the
legislative process were taking place, changes which
blended nicely with traditional procedures and humbly
accepted the myriad shackles imposed in the past. For
a time some of these developments were viewed as the
means to a legislative renaissance. This they were not,
but eventually out of them emerged the legislative council.

Notes

1. The literature on colonial backgrounds is diverse and extensive. Two of the basic general sources are: Charles M. Andrews, The Colonial Period in American History (4 vols.; New Haven: Yale University Press 1934-38), and Herbert L. Osgood, The American Colonies in the Seventeenth Century (3 vols.; New York: The Mac-Millan Co., 1904-07), and The American Colonies in the Eighteenth Century (2 vols.; New York: Columbia University Press, 1924). A few specifically pertinent items include Francis Newton Thorpe, Constitutional History of the United States (Chicago: Callaghan and Co., 1901), I; Oliver M. Dickerson, American Colonial Government 1696-1765 (Cleveland: A. H. Clark Co., 1912); Ralph V. Harlow, The History of Legislative Methods in the Period Before 1825 (New Haven: Yale University Press, 1917); Thomas F. Moran, The Rise and Development of the Bicameral System in America (Baltimore: Johns Hopkins University Press, 1895); Vernon L. Parrington, Main Currents in American Thought (New York: Harcourt, Brace and Co., 1927); Raymond G. Gettell, History of American Political Thought (New York: The Century Co. 1928); Andrew C. McLaughlin, The Foundations of American Constitutionalism (New York: New York University Press, 1932); Charles E. Merriam, A History of American Political Theories (New York: The MacMillan Co., 1915).

2. Alfred DeGrazia, Public and Republic (New York: Knopf, 1951), Ch. II-IV, sums up the evolution of American legislative concepts. See also Henry J. Ford, Representative Government, (New York: Henry Holt, 1924), Ch. IX and X; also L. F. Brown, "Ideas of Representation from Elizabeth to Charles II," Journal of Modern History, XI (1939), 23-40.

3. Thorpe, op. cit., p. 14.

4. Parrington, op. cit., I, 187.

5. Ibid., pp. 118-125, 233-247; DeGrazia, op. cit., p. 74; also Gettell, op. cit., pp. 57, 70; and Rossiter, op. cit., pp. 100-137.

6. Dickerson, op. cit., pp. 253-256.

18   The Legislative Council in the American States

7. Parrington, op. cit., p. 187.

8. Ibid., p. 160.

9. Moran, op. cit., pp. 51-53. Stevens traces bi-
cameralism in the colonial legislatures to "the colonial
tendency from the beginning of settlement on the Western
Continent . . . to follow the usage of the historic two
houses of the mother-land." Op. cit.. p. 84.

10. Harlow, op. cit., pp. 65, 116.

11. Ibid., pp. 2, 93, 113.

12. According to Dickerson, "probably no part of
our colonial experiences has had more permanent results than this constant subjection of local laws to the
review of the central government." Op. cit., p. 365.

13. Ivan Hinderaker, Party Politics (New York;
Henry Holt, 1956), p. 248.

14. Harlow, op. cit., pp. 79-80, 121.

15. Quoted passages are from John Locke, The Second Treaties of Civil Government, paragraphs 135 and
131, respectively.

16. Thorpe, op. cit., pp. 175-176.

17. Paul S. Reinsch, American Legislatures and
Legislative Methods (New York: The Century Co., 1907),
p. 129. Reinsch cites James Madison as describing
these two legislatures as "impotent" due to the existence
of the executive veto.

18. Caleb Perry Patterson, The Constitutional Principles of Thomas Jefferson (Austin: University of Texas
Press, 1953), pp. 87-88.

19. Three of the many sources which document this
trend are Simeon E. Baldwin, Modern Political Institu-
tions, Ch. III, "The First Century's Changes in Our
State Constitutions" (Boston: Little, Brown, and Co.,
1898), pp. 45-79; Reinsch, op. cit., esp. Ch. IV, "The
State Legislatures," pp. 126-158; and James Q. Dealey,
Growth of American State Constitutions, esp. Ch. III-VIII,
XV, XVII (Boston: Ginn and Co., 1915).

20. L. Q. C. Lamar, quoted in Frederick Jackson Turner, The Frontier in American History (New York: Henry and Co., 1920), p. 25.

21. Turner, ibid., p. 277.

22. Baldwin, op. cit., p. 59.

23. Ibid., p. 69. Also see Bryce, op. cit., I, 536, where he quotes the Secretary of the State of Nebraska as observing, "the public interests would be better served by having legislative sessions held only once every four years," and sums up with the observation that "the Americans seem to reason thus: 'Since a legislature is very far gone from righteousness, and of its own nature inclined to do evil, the less chance it has . . . the better . . . ; let us therefore prevent it from meeting.'"

24. They are analyzed by Baldwin, op. cit., pp. 45-79; and Dealey, op. cit., pp. 89-113 and 214-228. Also, see Reinsch, op. cit., p. 130.

25. Francis Newton Thorpe, The Federal and State Constitutions, Colonial Charters, and Other Organic Laws (Washington: Government Printing Office, 1909), III, pp. 1263-1292 and 1316-1358. See also, for an interesting analysis of constitutional development and growing legislative restraint, "The Story of Kentucky's Constitution," The Constitution of The Commonwealth of Kentucky (Frankfort: Legislative Research Commission, 1952), pp. 1-30.

26. Thorpe, ibid., Sections 27-58, 59, 190-218.

27. The Constitution of the Commonwealth of Kentucky, op. cit., pp. 3-4.

28. Ibid., p. 5.

29. Parrington, op. cit., II, 137.

30. Ibid., pp. 147-150.

31. Ibid., p. 150.

32. Ibid., pp. 151-154. The independent voting idea was not dear to Curtis alone, being espoused by such authorities as James Russell Lowell and reflected in the ephemeral Mugwump movement of 1884.

33. Quoted in Henry Steele Commager, The American Mind (New Haven: Yale University Press, 1950), p. 329.

34. Ibid., pp. 318-319.

35. Reinsch, op. cit., discusses and analyzes these developments; see esp. V., 127-128, 160-187, 231-256, 275-329.

36. Thorpe, Constitutions, II, 844.

37. Bryce, op. cit., I, 539-544.

38. Alexis de Tocqueville, Democracy in America, ed. by Phillips Bradley (New York: Knopf, 1945), I, 386.

39. Ibid., p. 414.

40. Ibid., p. 254.

41. Reinsch, op. cit., p. 155.

42. According to Reinsch, between 1877 and 1897 the number of House committees in Illinois more than doubled; by the end of the period the average member was on seven committees. A similar increase was noted in more than one-half of the states (p. 164). He further observed that in five years, 1899-1904, American state legislatures passed a total of 16,320 general laws (p. 300).

43. Herbert D. Croly, Progressive Democracy (New York: The MacMillan Co., 1914), p. 248.

44. Ibid., p. 250.

45. Dealey, op. cit., p. 163.

46. See, for example, A. E. Buck, The Reorganization of State Governments in the United States (New York: Columbia University Press, 1938), esp. pp. 3-37; Charles G. Haines, The Movement for the Reorganization of State Administration, the University of Texas Bulletin, Government Research Series No. 17 (Austin: University of Texas Press, 1920), esp. pp. 5-10, 59-64; Gustavus A. Weber, Organized Efforts for the Improvement of Methods of Administration in the United States (New York: D. Appleton and Co., 1919), esp. pp. 3-26; also, Dwight

Waldo, The Administrative State (New York: Ronald
Press, 1948), pp. 192-194.

47. Gettell, op. cit., pp. 549-555. See also Commager, op. cit., p. 399.

48. See, for example, Graves, op. cit., pp. 336-346;
and Leslie Lipson, The American Governor From Figure-
head to Leader (Chicago: University Press, 1939), esp.
Ch. IV and IX, dealing with the governor as chief legislator.

49. Buck, op. cit., p. 43. Buck's 227 page summary
of state reorganization plans fully or partly adopted between 1917 and 1937 contains only a half-page (p. 156)
on legislative reorganization—the adoption of the unicameral legislature by Nebrasks in 1934.

CHAPTER III

THE LEGISLATIVE REFERENCE BUREAUS

In the unexciting pages of contemporary session laws, one finds that nothing that is human is alien to the legislator.[1]

In the early days of the American republic "the organization of local communities . . . and the establishment of administrative authority" were the chief subjects of legislation.[2] But the 19th Century produced
fundamental changes in the content of the legislative process; it became necessary to legislate concerning a
prodigious range of subjects reflecting in their substance and their number the growing size and complexity
of society.

In New York the volume of legislative enactments
grew between 1830 and 1920 from about 60 acts a year to
almost a thousand. In the winter of 1906-07 forty-one
state legislatures passed 17,341 laws, out of about
80,000 bills introduced.[3] Yet the main modifications in
the legislative process had been proscriptive, and the
essential form of the legislative process was little
changed from Revolutionary times. The idea of the
"citizen legislator," the man of the people, certainly retained its vitality during a social transition in which
city dwellers rose from 7 percent to almost 50 percent
of total population,[4] and the gap between legislative myth
and legislative reality became tantamount to social
schizophrenia.

By the early 20th Century the state legislatures
were pretty much of a mess. In the 1917 Nebraska assembly, for example, 114 out of 803 House bills were

technically defective. Of 450 measures <u>enacted</u> by the
1915 New Jersey legislature, 81 were deficient. In 1902
the Ohio legislature inadvertently wiped out most of the
state supreme court's appellate jurisdiction, and a
$50,000 special session was necessary to repair the
damage. Chapter 75 of the Kansas Laws of 1911 was
repealed three times—twice by mistake—and two other
chapters were unwittingly and unnecessarily reenacted.
Between 1870 and 1913 the United States Supreme Court
ruled 200 statutory provisions unconstitutional, and in
one month the New York supreme court found 39 laws
passed in the previous five years to be unconstitutional.
In 1924 nearly half the appellate court litigation in the
United States involved the construction and/or constitutionality of statutes.[5]

The problem of the legislatures was one of both
method and substance. Long-established legislative procedures were simply not designed to cope with the volume and range of matters at hand. The public lamented
the lack of statesmanlike wisdom in the assemblies; the
legislators meanwhile struggled to exhaustion with the
process.[6]

Faint efforts were made to do something about this
state of affairs, first through the establishment of state
libraries offering reference materials[7] and later by the
invention of interim committees to give continuity to
legislative action and to study some of the complicated
questions of the day. The state libraries were not adequate means to the solution of legislative problems, however valuable they have proved in other respects. The
interim committees which appeared in New York and
Massachusetts early in the 20th Century have not been
sources of unmitigated joy, although they did mark the
beginning of efforts at advance preparation for legislating which produced the legislative reference bureaus
and laid some of the groundwork for the legislative

councils.[8] One of the surprising aspects of the American state legislatures through the first hundred years or so of their existence is the paucity of their own efforts to put their houses in order.

Most states continued well into the 20th Century to rely upon engrossing committees to review bills for technical defects prior to final passage. The arrangement was generally distinguished by its ineffectiveness.[9] The New York legislature in 1900 established a bill-drafting staff to help its members and to improve the technical quality of legislation. The step had originally been urged by the governor in 1885. In Great Britain as early as the 1870's practically all but private members' bills were being drafted by experts.[10] More than thirty years later the technical inadequacy of much legislation in many American states was little short of appalling. Industry and science, the corporation and the germ theory— these and a thousand other changes had modified the terms and tempo of government. And in the United States, in the 20th Century, some of the legislatures were beginning to attack the problem of how to better draft a bill.

"The Wisconsin Idea"

The Wisconsin Legislative Reference Library was established in 1901.[11] Its objective was the improvement of the quality of legislation through bill-drafting and reference assistance to legislators. The library was to function as a staff of technical experts for the legislators.[12]

The organization was created in the volant atmosphere of turn-of-the-century Wisconsin. It was an outgrowth of a lusty setting in which were mingled the spirit of the frontier, the unstereotyped creativity of a

state university dedicated to "adjusting pioneer ideals to
the new requirements of American democracy,"[13] and
a vital group of public-minded men led by such as John
R. Commons and Richard T. Ely. A Wisconsin graduate
student, Charles McCarthy, became the first head of the
Legislative Reference Library, the spirited leader of a
legislative reference "movement," and something of a
Wisconsin legend. In Madison today one still hears tales
of McCarthy and his "bill factory."[14]

    In the development of the Wisconsin Legislative Ref-
erence Library, "bill-drafting became one of the most
popular features of its work."[15] Technical assistance
in this phase of law-making was important both because
of the all-too-evident need and because of its popularity
among the legislators. But the "central main concept of
the legislative reference department," as McCarthy put
it, was something broader: it was to serve as "a body
of experts to gather information about the laws, to obtain statistics, to draft and redraft through the guidance
of the representatives of the people, laws which deeply
affect the people."[16] This implied a lot more than bill-
drafting and reference help for the individual legislator.
The basic aim of the bill factory was not the mere allevia-
tion of the difficulties of the solitary representative; this
was an effort to enable the legislature to come to grips
with its profoundly changing environment through the
focused study of important contemporary problems as
these became legislative issues.

    The Legislative Reference Library became the
means for tapping diverse talents available at the University of Wisconsin, and for gaining access to studies,
reports and experiences from all of America and much
of Europe.[17]

    Decades earlier, John Stuart Mill had suggested the
synthesis of the law-making expert and the legislative
representative:

> there is hardly any kind of intellectual work
> which so much needs to be done, not only by
> experienced and exercised minds, but by minds
> trained to the task through long and laborious
> study, as the business of law-making.[18]

Mill advocated delegation of the whole task of law drafting to an expert commission, leaving the representative
assembly to ratify or reject the measures drafted.[19]
McCarthy's thinking appears to have approached Mill's,
and it is likely that he was familiar with this classic 19th
Century treatise. Yet McCarthy was always—or almost
always—careful in his statements. Legislators have
ever been jealous of their status, if not their prestige,
and McCarthy took care to avoid the impression that his
was a brain-trust.[20]

John Stuart Mill may have helped inspire the invention of the Wisconsin Legislative Reference Library, and
through it the spread of the reference bureaus across the
states, but the legislative reference organizations were
based on no elaborate groundwork of theoretical argu-
ment and advocacy. No searching questions about the
basic concepts of the legislature were raised, nor would
they in all probability have been welcomed. Technical
service to the legislators in meeting practical needs
was the motif, and such rationale as developed around
the idea of the reference bureaus came later and was
both narrow and thoroughly concrete.[21]

McCarthy's bill factory was an institutional product
of our burgeoning economic and social development,
with its almost disastrous impact upon the state legislatures. It marked an emerging ability to recognize and
study practically and honestly the problems and needs
of the time. It involved no deep ideological concern
with forms and structures of government, nor did it
dwell wistfully upon the presumed merit of Godkin-like
legislatures. It assumed a synthesis of free opportunities

for free men with a government which was to foster and maintain the appropriate environment of this freedom.[22]

The Wisconsin Legislative Reference Library was a significant innovation in a tardy trend toward more effective state legislation. Unlike many such landmarks, it is an organization of more than historic interest. Served over the years by a succession of able directors, Herbert Ohm, Edwin Witte, and M. G. Toepel, it retains much of its original importance and elan.

The Spread of the Legislative Reference Services

Between 1907 and 1917 more than 30 legislative reference agencies were established, of which more than half survive. In 1907 alone Alabama,. Connecticut, Indiana, Michigan, Nebraska and the two Dakotas created legislative service agencies.[23] A fairly extensive literature on the organizations developed, most of it descriptive or laudatory or both.[24] In 1913 the American Bar Association's Special Committee on Legislative Drafting studied the general problem of legislative reference and bill-drafting services, arriving at the conclusion that

> the most important existing permanent public agencies for furnishing information and rendering expert assistance in the preparation of legislative enactments are the State legislative reference bureaus and drafting departments.[25]

As table one on page 33 suggests, legislative reference and bill-drafting services have continued to grow in number, although eleven states appear to have no formal arrangement for either bill-drafting or reference services or both. Several of these states, however, have

legislative council-type agencies which provide such
services in addition to others.

What the table does not indicate is that in a number
of the states listed the legislative reference and drafting agencies are limited organizations which furnish
little or nothing more than bill-drafting services.

Indiana is a case in point. It was one of the earliest
states to establish a Legislative Bureau. Its early directors were aggressive participants in the legislative
reference movement. The Indiana bureau, originally
under the direction of John A. Lapp and later of Charles
Kettleborough, had by 1917 established itself as a significant asset to the legislature.[26] It had become the statistical data collecting agency of the state, had developed a
special legislative library of about 10,000 items, was
drafting a considerable portion of the bills introduced in
the General Assembly, had published a series of ten research reports, was responsible for editing the state
Yearbook, and maintained a full-time professional staff
of three persons.[27] In 1924 Director Kettleborough tes-
tified that the services of the Indiana bureau had been
used by "every legislator for the past ten years."[28]

In 1955 the Indiana Legislative Bureau consisted of
an ailing attorney, a clerical employee, and a collection
of dusty bill files and law books.[29] Its only evident activities were bill-drafting before and during legislative
sessions, plus occasional responses to incidental legal
inquiries from legislators.[30] It had long ceased to
edit the state's Yearbook; it had even been dropped from
among the state agencies whose reports were contained
therein. Much of the legislative service work in the
state had been taken over by the Indiana State Chamber
of Commerce. The reference bureau had lost out to
executive leadership, the economy moves of the early
1930's, and a lack of legislative support. Only its bill-
drafting and bill-filing functions had secured lasting

acceptance. In the minds of the early leaders of the
bureau movement, however, drafting was a matter of
secondary importance. Policy-assistance work came
first. John A. Lapp had recommended that "the scheme
proposed years ago by John Stuart Mill be tried in connection with the legislative reference bureau in one of
the American states."[31]   Under this arrangement the
legislature would approve or disapprove the "principle"
of legislation, and the work of drawing up a statute would
be undertaken by a bill-drafting commission which would
have "absolutely no power over the policy of the bills,
but . . . would have complete authority over and responsibility for the form of the law."[32]

Such an arrangement would certainly have exceeded
the bounds of technical assistance reflected in bill-drafting procedures then in effect. Mill's intention was not
to limit the contribution of his expert commission to the
mechanics of law-making narrowly construed. Nor was
Lapp's, assuming he was serious about following Mill
(and thus not too serious about his "policy-form" dichotomy). After all, he was already deeply involved in the
mechanics of bill drafting.

Lapp was not optimistic about the prospects for his
brain-child, but thought the drafting departments of the
legislative reference agencies might develop into "something of this kind" if they ever overcame the handicap of
legislative suspicion over their possible usurpation of
legislative power. Sooner would the heavens fall. . . .

Only in a few places and to a limited extent did the
early legislative reference agencies make much of an
impact upon the substantive content of legislation, and it
was their efforts in this area that led to criticism.

During consideration of the establishment of a Congressional Legislative Reference Bureau a steady stream
of warnings was heard. Congress did not want a body
"to find conclusions for it."[33]   Chiefly to meet such

criticism, some of the leading spokesmen for the legislative reference agencies stressed the importance of an objective, non-recommendatory approach.

Charles McCarthy, whose sentiments regarding the role of the legislative reference agency are cited above, was certainly somewhat more—or less—than completely objective in his activities. At one point in his career he temporarily became a candidate for political office; one governor tried to destroy his reference library, and McCarthy's deft influence upon legislative matters during his tenure as legislative librarian in Wisconsin is not to be denied.[34] Yet in writing of his legislative reference work McCarthy cultivated the appearance of objectivity and avowed that "in a clerical capacity—I have tried gladly to carry out the will of the men of genius and power who composed the Wisconsin legislature."[35]

A few people faced up to this question of impartiality by admitting that at best it was an oversimplification of reality; "if the legislative reference bureau does not have a tendency to make for better legislation, there is no particular excuse for its existence."[36] But Freund and Luce expressed reservations about the prospects for any significant contribution from legislative reference agencies to the general elevation of substantive legislative standards and content.[37] In Leek's opinion, the bureaus had no choice but to cultivate the myth of objectivity as earnestly as they could. Exactness and scientific precision were his watchwords; he seemed convinced that practical distinctions could be made between facts and values, and that the future of the bureaus depended considerably upon their ability to hew to such lines.[38]

> . . . bill drafting, legislative reference, and statutory revision services have not fulfilled the high hopes expressed by their champions when they first attracted public attention.[39]

As the reference bureau movement spread it also
became dilute. The Wisconsin invention was copied but
its context could not be copied. The legislative reference bureaus were viewed increasingly in terms of
their mechanical contribution. In most states the original pressure to establish reference bureaus had come
from outside the legislatures. Once established, the
legislators had not sought more than technical help from
them. Jealous of prerogatives and afraid of their possible unsurpation, the lawmakers wrote no record of a
demand for policy assistance from the legislative reference bureaus. Reinsch had pointed out in the first book
on American legislatures that "the essence of legislative reference work is the furnishing of information. . . ."[40]
"No matter how efficient the technical services may be,
they cannot guarantee good legislation."[41]   Yet it was
chiefly in terms of technical services that the reference
bureau came by the 1920's

> to be so much an accepted part of governmental
> machinery that it is no longer the object of
> praise and attack that it was a few years ago.
> Like so many other structural reforms in
> government that were at first hailed as har-
> bingers of the millennium or condemned as
> destructive or subversive factors . . . the
> legislative reference bureau has realized
> neither the extravagant claims of its advo-
> cates nor the dire prophecies of its de-
> tractors.[42]

Thus the legislative reference services produced no
cure for our essential legislative ailments. Originally
conceived as potent means for improving the substantive
quality of legislation by getting the facts before the legislators, they evolved in most cases into bill drafting
staffs, to the disappointment of many early enthusiasts.
Perhaps the real failure here, if such there was,

consisted of a lack of wisdom and discernment on
the part of those who dreamed, rather than in the agencies which were the objects of those dreams. A careful
scrutiny of the following table will show that, although
the "reference movement" is a matter of history,
reference service has grown steadily, if unheralded,
over the years. Between 1937 and 1956 twenty-five
organizations were established in twenty different
states to perform one or more functions of the "ref-
erence-bureau type."

In this second phase of the Legislative Reference
movement almost as many organizations were established as in the pre-World War era of legislative-im-
provement-via-reference-services. The number of
states is somewhat less, however.

About half these recent reference-type agencies are
clearly limited to the performance of one or more technical functions such as bill drafting or statute revision.
But 13 of the group profess to be research organizations, and some of these are justly respected for the
quality and significance of their contributions to legislative policy-making.

Before discussing the latter-day establishment of
legislative reference and technical service organizations
some additional factors must be introduced. Here it is
sufficient to note that:

1. The continuing establishment and use of such
legislative service agencies is undeniable evidence of
the practical value of their functions. Long after the
impetus of reformist zeal had been lost agencies continued to be established whose antecedants were the
legislative references bureaus of the early 20th Century.

TABLE 1

REFERENCE-TYPE AGENCIES ESTABLISHED, 1937-1956

Year	Agency	Essentially Bill-Drafting & Related Functions	Broader Reference and Research Functions
1937	Illinois Legislative Council		
1937	Florida Statute Revision & Bill Drafting Depts.	*	
	Iowa Legislative Reference Bureau	*	
	North Carolina Div. of Legis. Drafting and Codification	*	
	Maine Legislative Research Committee		*
	Minnesota Revisor of Statutes	*	
1941	Michigan Legislative Service Bureau		*
1943	Missouri Legislative Research Committee		*
1944	Mississippi Revisor of Statutes	*	
1945	Alabama Legislative Reference Service		*
	Delaware Legislative Reference Bureau	*	
	North Carolina General Statutes Commission	*	
	New Jersey Bureau of Law & Legislative Reference		*

TABLE 1 — Continued

Year	Agency	Essentially Bill-Drafting & Related Functions	Broader Reference and Research Functions
1947	Connecticut Legislative Research Department	*	
	Maryland State Fiscal Research Bureau		*
	Minnesota Legislative Research Committee		*
1949	Florida Legislative Research Bureau		*
1951	Georgia Bill-Drafting Unit	*	
	Nevada Statute Revision Commission	*	
	South Dakota Revisor of Statutes	*	
1953	Colorado Legislative Council		*
	Massachusetts Legislative Research Bureau		*
	New Jersey Law Revision and Legislative Services Commission		*
	Oregon Legislative Counsel Committee	*	
1955	Iowa Legislative Research Committee		*

Source: Adapted from Book of the States, 1956-1957,
         pp. 122-123.

2. The greater success and appeal of these organizations has undoubtedly been in the field of technical assistance rather than legislative policy planning. The reasons for this are complex and an explanation at this point would be premature. It should be noted, however, that the original legislative reference agencies were for the legislatures—but not of them. Many of the bureaus were attached to state libraries, or simply created as independent governmental agencies. There was no systematic structuring of legislature-legislative reference bureau relations (except in connection with bill-drafting: some drafting agencies are responsible for the review of all proposed legislation for technical adequacy at some stage in the enactment process). In this respect some of the recent legislative reference agencies which engage in research on policy matters differ significantly from their antecedants.

3. The legislative reference agencies rested upon an inadequate set of assumptions about the nature of the legislative process. "Facts" and competent analysis—these alone are not the essence of legislating. "Get the facts and let the legislators decide" may be a neat and popular slogan, but it is not necessarily a valid assumption about the way in which laws are made.

> The legislator knows whereof he speaks, when he says that legislation based upon scientific knowledge is mostly myth. 'But why not reform?' the scientist queries. 'Why not build upon our knowledge instead of upon custom and gossip?' The legislator replies: 'What knowledge?'[43]

The knowledge upon which legislation is based is often subtle and complex. It may contain "elements which are intrinsic, not to the object studied, but to many other political considerations."[44] The character of legislative questions varies; some are highly technical and relatively "non-political." Others are the opposite, and many fall between the two extremes. Still others are both technically complex and charged with high political significance. One might arrange a rough but useful classification of some actual examples in some real legislature. It would undoubtedly indicate that the political significance of a question it not wholly evident upon its face. Thus merely improving the quantity and the quality of legislative fact-finding may be of quite limited value and pertinence to the process of legislative decision-making — a fact which was not recognized by many staunch exponents of the reference bureau.

4. Finally, as organizations — staffs established to serve the legislature and its individual members, functionally specialized and usually professionally competent — the reference bureaus were a significant innovation, the first of its kind to appear upon the American state legislative scene. In a fashion both fragmentary and uneven, these organizations and others which they inspired have made a very real contribution. Much of it — most of it, perhaps — has been in the realm of technical assistance, but in view of the great and ever-growing needs one finds here, hardly to be scorned for this reason. In a number of cases, reference and research agencies have contributed even more — they have contributed added quality to the substance of legislative decision-making.

Notes

1. Felix Frankfurter, The Public and Its Government (New Haven: Yale University Press, 1930), p. 29.

2. Ibid., p. 13.

3. J. H. Leek, Legislative Reference Work: A Comparative Study (Philadelphia: University of Pennsylvania, 1925), p. 33. This is the definitive study of legislative reference services to 1925.

4. Between 1830 and 1920.

5. Leek, pp. 14-19.

6. Reinsch, op. cit., pp. 306-307: "It has become physically impossible for a legislator to give careful reading to all the legislative bills . . . the work of the legislator ordinarily resolves itself to seeing that his own bills may receive a fair consideration. . . . It is therefore not surprising that our legislation should in general be hapharzard, inconsistent, and often absolutely incompatible."

7. Such establishments had existed since the early 19th Century in Massachusetts, New York, and New Jersey.

8. Regarding interim committees see Graves, pp. 245-249; Zeller, pp. 138-139, 185.

9. Massachusetts offered a possible exception to this statement. Here the rules committee of each house employed clerical help to assist members in initially drafting their bills. Robert Luce, Legislative Procedure (Boston: Houghton Mifflin, 1922), pp. 568-571.

10. Sir Courtenay Ilbert, Legislative Methods and Forms (London: Oxford University Press, 1901), pp. 90-91. The drafting office, that of Parliamentary Counsel to the Treasury, was permanently established in 1869.

11. Leek, op. cit., pp. 73, 77, 106-107. Pennsylvania had established a Legislative Reference Bureau in 1900, one year before Wisconsin. It was, however, a reference library in the traditional pattern.

12. See: Charles McCarthy, The Wisconsin Idea (New York: MacMillan & Co., 1912), esp. pp. 194-232.

13. F. J. Turner, op. cit., p. 287. For a glimpse of the spirit of the time and place, see: John R. Commons, Myself (New York: The MacMillan Co., 1934), esp. pp. 108-165. The Wisconsin Legislative Reference Library was part of a movement encompassing the whole of the government, including education, utility regulation, and labor legislation, which has been characterized as the "Progressive Movement." Much of its virtue lay in its

blend of practicality and principle. It was essentially pragmatic and concerned with immediate issues. Commons symbolized the movement, and epitomized its spirit. "In his pragmatism, his opportunism, his talent for compromise and for common sense, his shrewdness and curiosity, his humor and simplicity, his suspicion of theory and of theorists, his versatility and industry, and his idealism, Commons was one of the representative men of his generation." (Commager, op. cit., p. 57).

14. See, for example, M. G. Toepel, "The Legislative Reference Library: Serving Wisconsin," Wisconsin Law Review (January, 1951), p. 114.

15. McCarthy, op. cit., p. 57.

16. Ibid., pp. 213-214.

17. Ibid., p. 57. See also: F. J. Turner, op. cit., who observed that "even Western States like Wisconsin send commissions to study German and English systems of taxation, workingmen's insurance, old age pensions and a great variety of other remedies for social ills." (p. 294) This suggests the breadth of the Wisconsin idea as reflected in the aims of the Legislative Reference Library.

18. John Stuart Mill, Representative Government (London: Longmans, Green & Co., 1873), p. 39.

19. Ibid., Ch. V.

20. McCarthy, op. cit., pp. xiii-xiv.

21. See, for instance, Leek, op. cit., pp. 147-164.

22. F. J. Turner, op. cit., has an excellent statement of this theme, pp. 243-268.

23. Leek, op. cit., p. 58.

24. An extensive series of articles in the American Political Science Review, beginning in 1907 and running into the 1920's, included: E. A. Fisher, "Legislative Reference in the United States," III, 223-226; Ernest Bruncken, "Defective Methods of Legislation," III, 167-179; Ethel Cleland, "Legislative Reference" (survey), VII, 444-447, and X, 110-113; "Report of the Standing Committee on Legislative Methods," VIII, 271-280; Ernest

Bruncken, "Some Neglected Factors in Law Making,"
VIII, 222-237; Ethel Cleland, "Bill-Drafting," VIII, 244-
251; Ernest Freund, "The Problem of Intelligent Legislation," IX, 67-79; Ernst Freund, "Principles of Legislation," X, 1-19; Frank G. Bates, "Legislative Organization and Procedure," X, 120-123; and James A. Fairlie,
"Legislative and Municipal Reference Agencies," XVII,
303-308. Brief but frequent references will be found in
the files of the National Municipal Review from 1919 for-
ward. Leek's bibliography, at pp. 168-172, contains a
number of additional periodical items. Current tabular
information is available in the Book of the States, published biennially by the Council of State Governments,
Chicago, beginning in 1935.

25. The Problem of Legislative Reference and
Bill-Drafting Service, A Report of a Committee of the
American Bar Association (1913), reproduced in Weber,
op. cit., p. 313.

26. "Report of the Bureau of Legislative Information," Yearbook of the States of Indiana, 1917(Indianapolis: Wm. B. Burford, 1918), pp. 576-580.

27. Ibid.

28. Letter of Charles Kettleborough, December 16,
1924, quoted in Leek, op. cit., p. 128.

29. Interview, Mr. Herbert P. Kenney, Director,
1955.

30. Ibid.

31. John A. Lapp, "Making Legislators Law
Makers," Annals of the American of Political and Social Science, LIV (March, 1916), 172.

32. Ibid., pp. 173-174.

33. U. S. Congress, Senate, Report and Hearings on
a Legislative Reference Bureau, Sen. Report 1271, 62nd
Cong., 3rd Sess., (Washington: Government Printing
Office 1913), p. 116.

34. Interview with M. G. Toepel, Chief, Wisconsin
Legislative Reference Library, Madison, Wisconsin,
August 12, 1954. See also Leek, op. cit., p. 140, who

observes that Dr. McCarthy was the object of complaint as a result of "efforts to influence legislation."

35. McCarthy, op. cit., pp. xiii-xiv.

36. Letter of John A. Lapp, February 6, 1925, quoted by Leek, op. cit., p. 141. Some authorities admitted that not even bill draftsmen can wholly avoid questions of policy, in filling in details of legislative proposals, in dealing with what are ostensibly "forms" of legislation, and in generally attempting to draw lines between fact and value. See, for example, J. B. Kaiser, Law, Legislative Reference, and Municipal Reference Libraries (Boston: Boston Book Co., 1914), pp. 209-211.

37. Ernst Freund, Standards of American Legislation (Chicago: University of Chicago Press, 1917), p. 295; Robert Luce, Legislative Procedure (Boston: Houghton Mifflin Co., 1922), pp. 578-579.

38. Leek, op. cit., pp. 159-164.

39. Edwin E. Witte, "Technical Services for State Legislators," Annals of the American Academy of Political and Social Science, CVC (January, 1938), 141.

40. Ibid., p. 142. Reinsch's observation is in his American Legislatures and Legislative Methods at pp. 297-298.

41. Witte, op. cit., p. 141 (italics added).

42. J. H. Leek, "The Legislative Reference Bureau in Recent Years," American Political Science Review, XX (November, 1926), 823.

43. T. V. Smith, The Legislative Way of Life (1940, quoted in Alfred De Grazia, Public and Republic) New York: Knopf, 1951, p. 169.

44. De Grazia, Ibid.

TABLE 2

LEGISLATIVE REFERENCE AND BILL-DRAFTING AGENCIES IN THE UNITED STATES*

State	Agency	Date Established	Service: Reference Library	Bill Drafting	Statute Revision	Law and Bill Summaries	Spot Research	Research Reports
Alabama (a)	Legis. Reference Service	1945	*	*	*	*	*	*
California	Admin.-Legis. Reference Service (State Library)	1904	*				*	
	Legislative Counsel	1913		*	*			
Colorado	Legislative Reference Office (Dept. of Law)	1927	*	*	*	*	*	*
	Legislative Council	1953						
Connecticut (a)	Legis. Reference Dept. (State Library)	1907	*				*	
	Legis. Research Dept.	1947		*	*			
Delaware	Legis. Reference Bureau	1945	*	*	*		*	
Florida (a)	Legis. Research Bureau	1949	*			*	*	*
	Statutory Revision & Bill-Drafting Depts. (Office of Attorney General)	1939		*	*	*	*	
Georgia	State Library	1914	*				*	
	Bill Drafting Unit	1951		*		*	*	
Illinois	Legis. Reference Bureau	1913	*	*	*	*	*	
	Legislative Council	1937					*	*

TABLE 2 — Continued

State	Agency	Date Established	Service: Reference Library	Bill Drafting	Statute Revision	Law and Bill Summaries	Spot Research	Research Reports
Indiana	Legislative Bureau	1907	*	*	*	*		
Iowa	Legis. Reference Bureau	1939	*	*		*		
	Legis. Research Committee	1955					*	*
Kansas (a)	State Library	1909	*			*	*	
	Revisor of Statutes	1929		*	*	*	*	
Maine	Legis. Research Committee	1939		*	*	*	*	*
	Legis. Reference Section (State Library)	—	*			*	*	
Maryland (a)	Dept. of Legis. Reference	1916	*	*		*	*	
	State Fiscal Research Bureau (Dept. of Legis. Reference)	1947					*	*
	State Library	—	*					
Massachusetts	Legis. Research Bureau	1954					*	*
	Legis. Reference Division	1908	*				*	
	Counsel to Senate and Counsel to House of Representatives	—		*	*	*	*	
Michigan	Legis. Service Bureau	1941	*	*	*	*	*	*
Minnesota	Legis. Research Committee	1947	*				*	*
	State Law Library	—	*				*	

TABLE 2—Continued

State	Agency	Date Established	Service: Reference Library	Bill Drafting	Statute Revision	Law and Bill Summaries	Spot Research	Research Reports
Mississippi	Revisor of Statutes	1939		*	*	*	*	
	Revisor of Statutes (Dept. of Justice)	1944		*	*		*	
Missouri	Committee on Legis. Research	1943	*	*	*		*	*
Montana (a)	Legis. Reference Bureau (State Law Library)	1921	*					
Nebraska (a)	Revisor of Statutes	1945		*	*			
Nevada (a)	Statute Revision Commission	1951		*	*			
	Law and Legis. Reference Section (State Library)	—	*				*	
New Hampshire (a)	Legis. Service (State Library)	1913	*				*	
New Jersey	Law Revision and Legis. Service Commission	1954		*	*	*	*	*
	Bureau of Law and Legis. Reference (Division of State Library, Archives and History, Dept. of Education)	1945	*				*	*
New York	Legis. Reference Library (State Library)	—	*			*	*	
	Legis. Bill Drafting Comm.	—		*			*	

TABLE 2—Continued

State	Agency	Date Established	Service: Reference Library	Bill Drafting	Statute Revision	Law and Bill Summaries	Spot Research	Research Reports
North Carolina	General Statutes Commission (Department of Justice)	1945			*	*		
	Division of Legis. Drafting & Codification of Statutes (Department of Justice)	1939		*	*	*		
Ohio (a)	Legis. Reference Bureau	1910	*	*			*	
Oklahoma (a)	Legis. Reference Division (State Library)	1917	*	*		*	*	
Oregon	Legis. Counsel Committee	1953		*	*	*	*	
	State Library	1913	*				*	
Pennsylvania(a)	Legislative Reference Bureau	1900	*	*			*	
Rhode Island	Legis. Reference Bureau (State Library)	1907	*	*		*	*	
	Assistant in Charge of Law Revision (Office of Secretary of State)	—		*	*		*	
South Dakota(a)	Revisor of Statutes	1951		*	*			
Tennessee	State Library and Archives	—	*				*	
Texas	Legis. Reference Division (State Library)	1909	*	*(b)			*	

TABLE 2—Continued

State	Agency	Date Established	Service: Reference Library	Bill Drafting	Statute Revision	Law and Bill Summaries	Spot Research	Research Reports
Vermont	Legis. Reference Bureau (State Library)	1931	*	*	*	*	*	
Virginia	Division of Statutory Research and Drafting	1914	*	*	*	*	*	*
Washington	State Library	——	*				*	
Wisconsin	Legis. Reference Library	1901	*	*		*	*	*
	Revisor of Statutes	1909			*			
Wyoming (a)	State Library	——	*				*	

(a) Indicates state with legislative council which prepares recommendations for the legislature.
(b) Bulk of bill drafting is done by Attorney General's office as a courtesy to the legislature. Legislative Council and Legislative Reference Librarian also do some general drafting.

*Source: Adapted from "Permanent Legislative Service Agencies," The Book of the States, 1956-1957, op. cit., pp. 122-128.

CHAPTER IV

The 1920's — PREFACE AND PRELUDE

The first proposal for the establishment of legislative councils in American state government was made in 1919-20, by the National Municipal League. Thirteen years later the first legislative councils were created.

The early years of the 20th Century had produced the legislative reference bureaus, along with a variety of reforms in American state and local government. But the movement from reference bureau to legislative council was neither direct nor simple. It was bound up with the renaissance of reform after World War I, and with the emergence of a new agency for the strengthening of state government— the American Legislators' Association, which evolved into the Council of State Governments. It was affected by the lively pursuit of governmental improvement spurred by the late Charles E. Merriam, and was perhaps influenced by the creation of a proto-council in Wisconsin by Governor Philip La-Follette. Out of all this came first the moribund Michigan Legislative Council; largely independent of these efforts of the 1920's another legislative council was created in Kansas. In the 1930's two streams merged— the thought and action which had led to the Michigan council and the mutation which had occurred in Kansas jointly produced what has come to be called the "legislative council movement."

The League and the Council

The National Municipal League, created in 1894,
served as coordinator for a variety of voters leagues,
citizens leagues, committees and similar organizations
interested in local and state government improvement.
These in turn were the protagonists of a striking series
of reforms which included the short ballot, executive
budget, city manager form of government, improved governmental personnel administration, direct election of
senators, the initiative and referendum, and other items.
The League was part of a universe which included the
Proportional Representation League, the National Popular Government League, and the National Short Ballot Organization.[1] In 1919 and 1920 the National Municipal
League sponsored the first American proposal for a
legislative council. The manner in which this proposal
was formed is a wry and curious tale.

In December, 1919, the National Municipal Review
published a preliminary draft of the "Proposed Provisions of a Model Constitution" for submission to the
Moot State Constitutional Convention which was held in
Cleveland, Ohio, on December 29-31.[2] This draft had
been prepared by a committee whose members included
professors Harold W. Dodds and Arthur W. Holcombe.
Mr. Richard S. Childs, representing the National Short
Ballot Organization, was apparently the guiding figure
behind the most radical aspect of the proposal——the establishment of a state manager form of government.

The draft provided for a unicameral legislature,
meeting biennially and elected by the Hare system of proportional representation. The governor was to be
elected from among the legislators, and was to have
neither veto nor appointive power. An administrative
manager was to be selected by the legislative branch,
for an unfixed term of office, at a salary of $10,000 per

year, to assume full responsibility for the administration of the state. Policy-wise, the legislature was to be supreme, and its supremacy was to be exercised through a body entitled the "Legislative Council."

> Legislative Council. The legislature at the beginning of the session of 1921 and of each biennial session thereafter, shall elect from its own members in the manner hereinafter provided a legislative council of nine members.
>
> Powers of Legislative Council. The legislative council shall have power to prepare and introduce legislation, to make inquiries with powers of subpoena into matters affecting the general welfare; to appoint and remove the administrative manager; to supervise and direct the work of the administrative manager; to appoint the civil service commission as hereinafter provided.
>
> The Legislative Council shall be the only committee of the legislature. Any member of the legislature may at any time file a bill with the legislative council, and within fifteen days, if the legislature is not in session, the legislative council shall prepare a report thereon, and such report and the bill shall be printed forthwith and delivered to the members of the legislature. No bill may be introduced in the legislature except by the legislative council, or by a majority vote of the legislature after the legislative council has reported on it.
>
> Governor. The chairman of the legislative council shall be that member who receives the largest number of first choice votes at the selection of the council . . . and shall be entitled governor. He shall have no veto or appointive power.
>
> The Administrative Manager. The legislative council first elected under this constitution shall appoint an administrative manager. . . .[3]

At the Cleveland conference the council-manager plan was rather thoroughly beaten down, along with some of its supporters. Charles A. Beard led the opposition. He urged "the necessity for political leadership in the executive," and favored the creation of a strong governor.[4]

At the Cleveland meeting a committee was appointed to redraft the proposed model constitution to reflect the strong governor position. The results were published in November, 1920.[5] A unicameral legislature meeting annually and elected under the Hare system was proposed, with a governor empowered to participate in legislative sessions but not to vote. The legislative council, key element of the first draft, was retained by the process of warping it into the new structure.

The governor was made an <u>ex officio</u> member (though not necessarily chairman) of the council, which was

> to collect information concerning the government and general welfare of the state and to report thereon to the Legislature. . . ; to prepare such legislation and make such recommendations thereon to the Legislature in the form of bills or otherwise as in its opinion the welfare of the state may require. . .[6]

and to study and report on measures submitted to it by the governor or members of the legislature.

The council was intended "to furnish much needed leadership in legislation and to exercise on behalf of the legislature proper supervision over administrative affairs."[7] At Indianapolis in December, "a good-sized majority" of the delegates voted in favor of the legislative council proposal set forth in the committee draft.[8] In other matters they tended to favor traditional patterns of organization; proportional representation, unicameralism and the legislative council were the only <u>avant garde</u> elements of their legislative proposals.[9]

The carry-over of the council proposal from the
1919 to the 1920 drafts amounted to transubstantiation.
In the heroic first draft the council was the focal point
of a government characterized by legislative supremacy.
In the retreat toward reality which later took place, the
whole approach was inverted, but the remains of the council
idea carried over. In the first draft the council structure
and functions had been sharply delineated. In the second they were more generally sketched, although the intent seems clear: the council was to be the focus of
legislative planning and leadership.

The second proposal probably did not reflect an assumption that the council would serve in lieu of all other
legislative committees. But was it assumed that members of the legislature would, perhaps by serving on a
full-time basis, undertake the council's duties, or were
they to be assisted by a professional staff of researchers?
More than a quarter of a century later the question is not
exactly compelling. It is germane to this extent: the
lack of definition at this point suggests that a significant
characteristic of the council concept as it developed at a
later date had been ignored.

In its carry-over the legislative council idea lost its
original meaning but remained a provacative suggestion
for strengthening state legislatures which was unques-
tioningly accepted by the progress-minded members of
the 1920 National Municipal League convention, even
though most of them must have been quite unfamiliar
with the whole idea.

Its only direct antecedent was the proposal made
three-quarters of a century earlier by John Stuart Mill.

Mill had approached the subject of representative
government in terms of the problem of effectively putting
together the need for popular representation and "the
great advantage of the conduct of affairs by skilled persons, bred to it as an intellectual profession."[10]   The

ultimate controlling power must rest in the people, and
Mill accepted the idea of the amateur "citizen legislator."[11] But he recognized that this left a series of basic
questions unsettled, including "what actual functions,
what precise part in the machinery of government, shall
be directly and personally discharged by the representative body?"[12]

The function of the legislature was to be deliberation, inquiry, and the continuing ratification of the conduct of government. There would also be a small body,
"a Commission of legislation, having for its appointed
office to make the laws."[13] The representative assembly would pass upon these laws. It would also possess
power to refer any subject to the Commission, "with
directions to prepare a law."[14] All bills would, of course,
be drawn by this commission.

Mill's structure and the legislature envisioned in
the first draft of the Model State Constitution were similar with one essential exception: Mill's commission
would have been an expert body; the council of the model
constitution draft would have been chosen from among
the legislators.

The initially proposed legislative council would have
resembled a legislative cabinet, with the line between
executive and legislative branches drawn in terms of a
policy-administration dichotomy. The second council
proposal suggested an effort to balance forces by strengh-
ening the legislature in a context in which both executive
policy leadership and legislative policy-making were
avowed and accepted.

To overemphasize the direct influence of either John
Stuart Mill or the Model State Constitution upon the development of the legislative councils in the American
states would be misleading. The League's legislative
council proposal created no great stir, and it received
little attention once the model constitution was published.

A single lonely article in 1926 represents the only critical attention given the legislative council proposal during
the period between 1921 and 1933.[15] Meanwhile, the National
Municipal Review continued through the 1920's to document the ineptitude and ineffectiveness of our state legislatures.

Henry W. Toll and the A.L.A.

Two notable developments of the 1920's and early
1930's are pertinent, in their respective ways, to the development of the legislative councils. The first of them
was the creation, in 1925, of the American Legislators'
Association, under the aegis of Henry W. Toll, lawyer,
business executive and Colorado state legislator. The
second was the establishment in 1931 of an "Executive
Council" linking the governor and legislature of the
state of Wisconsin.[16]

The Wisconsin council was in its way a prototype of
the legislative council. The American Legislators' Association was the forerunner of the Council of State Governments, a key organization in the spread of the legislative council idea during part of the past quarter-
century.

Henry W. Toll had entered the Colorado Senate in
1923. He was appalled by the inadequacy of the legislative process and concerned over its long-run consequences to state government. In the best American
tradition he set out to do something about the situation,
convinced of the need for a nation-wide effort to elevate
both the status and competence of the legislatures. His
idea was the formation of a non-partisan association
"in which the legislators would work together for the
purpose of improving legislative standards and personnel
throughout the country."[17]

The response to that idea is one of those occasional
sparkling illustrations of the way in which, under fortunate circumstances, a single man may mould an institution and make a little dent in history. Toll, armed
with his checkbook and a sense of purpose, helped create
the Council of State Governments. His approach was
pragmatic; his postulates were few and simple: the
need for improving the legislatures by the interstate ex-
change of information, the promotion of state legislative
reference bureaus, and the enhancement of the dignity
and status of legislators and legislatures.[18]

In 1925 all of this was but an idea. By 1927 it
seemed to be a dead dream: 7,500 people were invited
to a meeting of the ALA; six appeared—Mr. Toll, four
reporters, and a lobbyist.[19] In 1930 new life appeared in
the form of additional funds granted by the Spelman Fund,
which supported a new magazine, increased an expanded
drive for membership, and the transfer of headquarters
from Denver to Chicago.

The move to Chicago brought the ALA under the
aegis of perhaps the most scintillant approach of its
time to the continuing study and reform of American
government, the Political Science Department of the
University of Chicago and its missionary-chairman,
Charles E. Merriam. Henry Toll became one member
of a group of dedicated reformers. His organization became an early affiliate of the Public Administration
Clearing House,[20] and a member of the cluster of agencies now identified as the "1313" group which share headquarters at 1313 East 60th Street, Chicago.[21]

The specific contributions of the Council of State
Governments to the spread of legislative councils among
the American states have been many; most of them came,
however, after the "council movement" had gained considerable impetus. The ALA and its successor organization, the Council of State Governments, did not adopt

the proposals of the 1920 Model State Constitution as part
of its own program; the League itself had not placed much
emphasis upon them. Legislative reference bureaus were
still regarded as a most likely way to improve the quality
of the legislative product.

Yet there was a certain prescience in the fact that
one of the close associates of Toll and Merriam at
Chicago was a man named Guy Moffat, a representative
of the Spelman Fund. Without Moffat's support, and without Spelman Fund research grants from 1933 to 1937,
the Kansas Legislative Council would'probably have
failed. Had this happened there would have been no legislative councils to assist and encourage in the 1930's and
after.

The Wisconsin Executive Council

In Wisconsin, birthplace of the legislative reference
bureau, a prototype of the legislative council appeared
with the creation of the Executive Council in 1931. This
council was not intended to supplant the Legislative Reference Library; it was a different type of organization,
and it is in terms of this difference that the Executive
Council first approximated the character of the legisla-
latiye council.

The Wisconsin council consisted of a continuing
committee of twenty members, ten legislators appointed
in the same manner as members of standing committees,
and ten citizens appointed by the governor.[22] Its functions were "the preparation of programs prior to the
meeting of the legislature, in order to expedite public
business and better prepare material for legislative discussion,"[23] the continuous review of state administration, and "the bringing of responsible leaders drawn from
different major interests in the state into consultation

with the governmental leaders of the state."[24] The council was to render continuing advice to the governor, who set forth the reasoning behind the arrangement in these unusual terms:

> These proposals would, in my judgment, give a
> better opportunity for the continuous review of
> the activities of government in this state. They
> offer us a safeguard against hasty, arbitrary,
> and ill-informed development of policy. They
> are an alternative to the drift toward extend-
> ing arbitrary powers to the governor and the
> executive branch of government without some
> compensating controls. . . .[25]

Here was the governor of Wisconsin recommending the establishment of an executive-legislative-interest group policy planning body as a means of mitigating a trend toward executive domination of policy-making! One does not often find instances of this sort.

The Wisconsin council anticipated the later legislative councils in the sense that both are essentially concerned with planning as a basis for policy-making. It was not simply a fact-finding body. Interest group representation within it attests to this, and incidentally distinguishes it from the typical legislative council.

The Wisconsin Executive Council depended for its success upon gubernatorial support. Governor LaFollette was defeated for renomination in 1932 and the council declined, although "there was a kind of residue in the Division of Departmental Research in the Executive Office of the Governor which has played an important part in recent years."[26] By this time, however, the true legislative council had been established and was already beginning to spread across the states.

Thus we come to the 1930's. Over the span of a hundred and fifty years the very purposes and fabric of state government had changed. The legislatures had

changed, too, but in much of the process of legislating
sameness rather than change was the striking characteristic. The context had changed far more than the
assemblies. A horse and buggy is a horse and buggy,
but a horse and a buggy on a 19th Century turnpike is
different from a horse and a buggy on a six lane super-
highway.

Actual changes in the legislative process had been
largely technical or mechanical, ranging from the voting
machines first adopted in Wisconsin in 1917[27] to the
legislative reference movement, which succeeded largely
in its bill-drafting aspect.[28] Some spread in the use of
interim commissions reflected a spasmodic and fragmentary effort at more systematic legislation; the establishment of the American Legislators' Association and the
Council of State Governments was an attempt to strength-
en the legislative process in a general way.

The states and the system of American government
were the products of vision and imagination; a fact which
by the 1930's was but poorly reflected in their legislatures. By the test of survival one must judge the legislatures viable. By the criterion of significance one
must rank them high, despite the vicissitudes of a century and a half. Beyond this, however, the picture is
not bright. One reasoned resume of the ailments and
inadequacies of the state legislatures in the early 1930's
cited the following defects and problems, at the same
time acknowledging that "they are bodies of supreme
importance in our schemes of government."[29] Note how
many of the following remarks remain pertinent a quarter of a century later:

1. On the whole, the individuals who serve in the
legislatures "do not have the experience or training
which their onerous duties require." Most are amateurs,
novices, who serve too short a time to really learn their
business, who "come and go so rapidly that continuity of

policy, collective knowledge and professional standards cannot develop into what they should be."[30]

2. The size of many of the state legislatures is so great that they are unwieldy.

3. Infrequent sessions, short sessions and poor pay, reflecting the assumption that the legislatures are an evil in themselves, contribute to the inadequacy of many of the state legislatures.

4. Continued reliance upon geography as a basis for the apportionment of representatives has given rural areas a disproportionate voice in legislation; antiquated public and legislative attitudes toward lobbying both reflect legislative tendencies toward unrepresentativeness and are completely ineffectual.

5. "We have clung to the notion that our law makers can operate as amateurs;"[31] the consequences of this assumption and its application have been to leave the legislatures without staff facilities and dependent upon lobbyists in their efforts to deal with complex and technical matters.

6. Bicameral legislative organization fosters irresponsibility, in addition to being unnecessarily complex and expensive. "It is curious how completely standardized our state governments are."[32]

7. Finally, our system of separation of powers and executive independence has conspired "to make legislative positions of secondary or even of minor political importance. . . and to relegate the legislator to the role of criticism or negation in the formulation of public policy."[33]

A hundred and fifty years after the founding of the Republic, the nation, in the depths of depression, moved into a new era marked by potent pressures toward centralization—pressures ascribed by some to the inadequacy and incompetence of the states. There were no applied developments in the organization and operations of the American state legislatures that appeared to promise improvement commensurate with the magnitude of the tasks and needs confronting the assemblies.[34]

Notes

1. For a review of the organizations and their efforts, with particular stress upon the National Municipal League, see: Richard S. Childs, Civic Victories (New York: Harpers, 1952); and Frank M. Steward, A Half Century of Municipal Reform (Berkeley: University of California Press, 1950).

2. "Proposed Provisions of a Model Constitution," National Municipal Review, VIII (December, 1919), 706-723.

3. Ibid., pp. 707-708.

4. Ferdinand H. Glaser, "Our Moot State Constitutional Convention," National Municipal Review, IX (January, 1920), 67.

5. "Proposals for Model State Constitution. Progress Report of Committee on State Government," National Municipal Review, IX (November, 1920), 711-715.

6. Ibid., p. 711.

7. Editors note, ibid., p. 691.

8. Ferdinand H. Glaser, "Our Annual Meeting at Indianapolis," National Municipal Review, X (January, 1921, 10.

9. Mill, op. cit., p. 47.

10. Ibid., p. 47.

11. Ibid., pp. 35, 47.

12. Ibid., pp. 35-36.

13. Ibid., p. 40.

14. Ibid., p. 41.

15. Howard White, "Relations Between the Governor

and the Legislature in the Model Constitution," National
Municipal Review, XV (August, 1926), 441-444.

16. For a description of the Wisconsin council, see
the note by Gaus, "The Wisconsin Executive Council,"
American Political Science Review, XXVI (October, 1932),
914-920.

17. "The History of the Council," The Book of the
States, 1937 (Chicago: The Council of State Governments),
pp. 8-13, summarizes the development of the American
Legislators' Association. The above quotation is at
page 8. See also W. Brooke Graves, Uniform State Action (Chapel Hill: University of North Carolina Press,
1934), pp. 57-61.

18. An early statement of the purpose of the American Legislators' Association will be found in State Government, III (April, 1930), 12-14.

19. Book of the States 1937, p. 8.

20. An óbject of the ALA was defined as: "To assist in the development of the public Administration
Clearing House and in other efforts to coordinate work
being done to improve government." "The Horizon in
1930, or the Project of the American Legislators' Association," State Government, III (April, 1930), 14.

21. The story of P.A.C.H. and the "1313," group is
nowhere better told than in the autobiography of its pro-
genitor, the much-loved Louis Brownlow. See A Passion
for Anonymity, The Autobiography of Louis Brownlow,
Second Half (Chicago: University of Chicago Press,
1958), esp. pp. 228-291.

22. This description is drawn from Gaus, op. cit.
Another brief discussion of the Wisconsin council is to
be found in Carroll H. Wooddy, "The Legislature:
Watch-Dog or the House-Dog?," State Government, IV
(June, 1931), 12-13.

23. Gaus, op. cit., p. 917.

24. Ibid.

25. Message of Philip F. LaFollette, Governor of
Wisconsin, to the Wisconsin Legislature, Thursday, January 15, 1931, quoted in ibid., p. 916.

26. Letter from John M. Gaus, November 14, 1956.

27. Alice Kelly, "Flash Voting, " State Government,
III (October, 1930), 6-8. According to Miss Kelly, "in
Wisconsin, the legislature has at no time been less than
unanimously in favor of the new system, which it regards
as perhaps the greatest stride in modern legislative
procedure"(p. 8).

28. Perhaps an explicit reference to the unicameral
movement might be added here, although this was, of
course, a feature of the Model State constitution. A
summary of the development of the unicameral movement will be found in John P. Senning, The One-House
Legislature (New York: McGraw-Hill, 1937), esp. Ch. II,
"The Unicameral Movement in the Several States," pp.
39-49.

29. Albert W. Atwood and Joseph McGoldrick,
"What is the Matter with the State Legislatures?,"
Government Series III, (Lecture No. 10, delivered March
7, 1933, over the Network of the National Broadcasting
Company), (Chicago: University of Chicago Press, 1933),
pp. 1-11. The following quotations are from this source.

30. Ibid., p. 3. Accompanying figures indicated
that 40% to 50% of the total seats in the state legislatures were regularly being vacated each two years.

31. Ibid., p. 6.

32. Ibid., pp. 8-9.

33. Ibid., p. 10.

34. The attitude is to be noted even in Graves, Uniform State Action, in his evaluation of the prospects for
alternatives to centralization at the national level. See,
for example, pp. 290-291, 303-304. At p. 304 he observes: "The states have not lost a single power of
which they made effective use. The powers they have
lost have been powers that they either could not or would
not use. . . . The situation can be changed if the states
generally will become as alert in the discharge of their
duties and responsibilities as they ought to be, and as
the Federal government frequently is." See also: William Yandell Elliott, The Need for Constitutional Reform

(New York: Whittlesey House, 1935), esp. pp. 191-192;
and Jane Perry Clark, The Rise of a New Federalism
(New York: Columbia University Press, 1938), p. 319.

CHAPTER V

KANSAS: THE FIRST SUCCESSFUL
LEGISLATIVE COUNCIL

In 1933 the scene shifts to Kansas. The Kansas
Legislative Council was the first of a series of bodies to
be established under the label of legislative council. Its
invention was consistent with American Legislative and
political traditions, and it soon became a model for later
councils.

It all began with Sam Wilson.[1] A civil engineer who
became temporary manager of the Greater Dayton (Ohio)
Association, Sam Wilson was instrumental in a landmark
event in American city government—the adoption of Dayton's city manager charter. Working with Dr. A. R.
Hatton, a leading figure in city charter reform, Wilson
later managed city manager charter campaigns in San-
dusky, Ohio, and Lockport, New York. In 1927 he helped
lead the first of two reform movements culminating in
the eventual clean-up of Kansas City, Missouri.

Wilson became manager of the Kansas State Chamber
of Commerce in 1929. About this time the chamber began an extensive state tax study which produced a number of important proposals for tax law changes. Within
the chamber and its tax study committee the results of
the study were educational. Within the legislature they
were nil.

In 1931 a nine-man tax study group was organized
and another study was started. The committee included
three technicians— Jens Jenson, Camden Strain, and
Harold Howe, plus six members of the state chamber.
The first meeting of this group was not altogether

successful. According to Wilson, the technicians were
"looking west, and the business men were looking east."

During a year and a half of study and discussion a
synthesis was reached. The lay members came to understand a great deal about the technical complexity of
taxation, and the technicians acquired a grasp of practical considerations and lay viewpoints. Wilson was im-
pressed by the shaping of thought and opinion which
seemed to accompany this long-term study and deliberation, particularly the gradual adoption by the technicians
and laymen of attitudes which represented adjustment for
both. The result of the work was a set of solid proposals
backed by thorough analysis.

While the study was underway Wilson became dis-
couraged. "What hope could we have before the legislature when it takes us more than a year to swing into a
position— and the legislature only meets for sixty days?"

Wilson thought about this problem in terms of his
experience in the State Chamber of Commerce.

> Our work was usually done through study com-
> mittees which then reported to the Board of
> Directors. The board had the responsibility
> of passing upon the work and the recommen-
> dations of its committees. The committees
> themselves, as evidenced by the tax study
> group, worked rather steadily over long
> periods of time, to assimilate material and
> formulate proposals upon the basis of care-
> ful study and consideration. The legislature,
> on the other hand, was bombarded with any-
> where from 800 to 1,000 different proposals
> on almost as many subjects in a biennial
> sixty-day session. How could the gradual,
> subtle process of shaping judgments and
> opinions on the basis of careful considera-
> tion take place in this hectic environment?

Wilson set about seeking "something which in terms
of results would be similar to our approach in the chamber." He had seen the product of one two-year study go
down the drain and quite concerned about the prospect
that the same thing might happen to the work of the new
tax study committee. Why not establish in the legislature
a group of committees, supported by a research staff, to
scrutinize problems and formulate recommendations during the interim between biennial sessions? In the spring
of 1932 Wilson talked with Willard Breidenthal, a personal friend and an influential Kansas Democrat, who reacted favorably to this idea.

Soon afterward Wilson approached Roy Bailey, a Republican newspaper editor and an active member of the
Kansas Chamber of Commerce. After an afternoon of
discussion Bailey expressed an encouraging opinion of
the idea.

Next, Wilson arranged a meeting with the head of
the University of Kansas Political Science Department,
Dr. Frederick Guild. Guild was familiar with the work
of the American Legislators' Association and had considerable knowledge of the operation of state legislatures. He made a number of suggestions, offered his
help, and urged Wilson to go ahead with his plan.
Shortly after this

> Dr. A. R. Hatton came to Washburn College,
> Topeka, to deliver a speech. I was eager for
> the chance to discuss this matter with him, and
> he was most encouraging. He referred to the
> Model State Constitution, which was the first
> time I knew that the idea had ever been con-
> sidered.
>
> Then we had another break. On the State Cham-
> ber of Commerce Board were some men ex-
> perienced in the legislature. One of these, Will
> Vernon, was both a member of the legislature
> and a member of the Board of Directors of the

state chamber—the only board member in the
legislature.

By now it was October, 1932. The State Chamber of
Commerce Board was meeting in Wichita. The next session of the legislature was only a few months off. Wilson
discussed his idea with Will Vernon and Vernon expressed a desire to "carry the ball with the directors."
The Board of Directors of the state chamber approved
the proposal for a legislative policy organization, and
Vernon indicated his intention to support the matter in
the coming session.

In January, Vernon was elected Speaker of the
House. In February a bill embodying the substance of
the idea was introduced in the Senate, based upon a two-
page memo prepared by Camden Strain after discussions
with Guild and others, outlining the essentials of such a
project.

Meanwhile, a member of the House had obtained Governor Alf Landon's support for legislation to create a
continuing interim commission on taxation, to be patterned after a similar body in New York State. This plan
was not entirely dissimilar to the Wilson-Vernon proposal, and conflict and overlapping might have resulted
from adoption of both bills. The Governor had already
used a certain amount of influence to move the tax study
bill along in the House.

"But, after a discussion, Governor Landon told me
that he would do nothing further—he would not do anything for our proposal, or against it." The tax study bill
had passed the House. "It was pretty well set in the Senate, and had been referred to the committee which had
our bill. At this point the prospect for the council bill
looked rather dim." Wilson continues:

I called a man of considerable political influence, Frank Haucke, a former candidate

for Governor. He was also a director of the
State Chamber of Commerce. He came up and
saw the Senate committee chairman privately,
and our bill came out of committee first.

Will Vernon and I knew we couldn't get the bill
through with any adequate appropriation for research. We found ourselves in a position where
we considered we had either to take a chance on
getting research work from other sources, or
else were going to lose our bill. We decided to
take the chance.

After a rather lively fight in the Senate the legislative council bill was passed, with no research appropriation. The act was signed by the Governor on March 13,
1933, and became effective the next day. The first members of the Kansas council were appointed shortly thereafter.

At the first council meeting after the legislative session there was a discussion of the problem of inadequate
school facilities in Kansas. Camden Strain, research
director of the State Chamber of Commerce, had been
conducting a survey in this field. The council named a
committee to look into the matter. The committee
turned to Wilson, and Camden Strain was temporarily
loaned to the council to continue his work. More than
twenty years later he was still with the Kansas Legislative Council as assistant director.

Wilson had maintained his contact with Dr. Guild
during the time when the organization and operation of
the council were under consideration. Guild had suggested that a foundation such as the Spelman Fund might
conceivably furnish money for the initial financing of a
council research program. Following enactment of the
council statute Guild contacted the Spelman Fund. Shortly after the initial council meeting, Guy Moffat, the Spel-

man Fund executive, appeared at Wilson's office. After
discussions the Fund agreed to make a $15,000 research
grant to the Kansas Legislative Council.

Following this, a council committee met to consider
organization of a research staff. Sam Wilson was invited to attend the meeting. He recalls that there was
"some difficulty." "One politician was going to get one
of his friends into the job [of research director]."

At this point Wilson told the group: "I don't know if
Santa Claus is coming next year. But if any bottlenecks
get into this, I am going to see that Santa Claus doesn't
come next year." The council committee deferred action upon the appointment of a research director and
authorized the Lieutenant Governor to make staffing arrangements. He in turn delegated the job of finding a
research director to Vernon and Wilson who logically
recommended Fred Guild.

The selection of Dr. Guild was the final piece of
good fortune in this story. Twenty-one years later, in
talking of the matter, Wilson said "We had a lot of luck;
and our biggest piece of it was Fred Guild. The wrong
man could have wrecked it—and wrecked it forever."

Many years after these initial steps had been taken,
W. Brooke Graves observed:

> It has often been said that an institution is but
> the lengthened shadow of a man. The council
> movement is what it is largely because of the
> character of Frederick H. Guild, because of
> his courage and devotion to an idea. He has
> not only contributed greatly to the success of
> the Kansas Council, which he helped to es-
> tablish, but he has had a profound influence
> upon the development of councils in other
> states. It has become standard practice for
> states working on council legislation to send
> a delegation to visit "the sage of Topeka."[2]

Prior to the establishment of the legislative council Kansas had made occasional use of interim committees, as many as two per biennium.[3] Out of this experience had come no impetus toward a broader, more permanent arrangement of the type represented by the council. Kansas had also developed something more than merely nominal legislative reference facilities in the Kansas State Library. For years the library had maintained legislativè bill files, a special vertical file reference collection, an elaborate clipping service, and current information on a variety of legislative subjects. It was— and is—in a position to produce "information on a large number of subjects. . . . It is not in a position to compile or tabulate or analyze this material."[4] This legislative reference service had been in existence since 1909.[5] It had been no source of impetus toward a broader legislative service agency, and its continued existence has evidently posed no real problems of conflect or duplication of function vis-a-vis the council.

The Kansas legislature and its leaders could claim little credit for the establishment of the Kansas council. There is a degree of irony in the fact that a state chamber of commerce, rather than the National Municipal League or some political scientist versed in the nuances of the legislative process and the writings of John Stuart Mill, must be credited with the establishment of the first successful American legislative council. The directness and simplicity of the approach were a vivid testament to its underlying pragmatism. In this sense, at least, the establishment of the Kansas council was compatible with the pattern of development which has marked the whole history of the American state legislature.

In a relatively short time the Kansas council became securely established. During the first four years of its existence "many legislators were very critical," feeling that "the council would attempt to dictate policy to the legislature. The council barely survived in the 1935 and 1937 sessions."[6] In both these sessions bills to abolish the council were seriously considered. No such proposals have been made since 1939.

The council's early years were not marked by gubernatorial hostility, a fact which Dr. Guild regards as significant. "Probably no legislative council could long endure if its program were constantly to be opposed to that of the governor."[7]

The pristine quality of the statute establishing the Kansas Legislative Council is worthy of note.[8] In a quarter of a century only one minor amendment proved necessary. The original act had required that the minority party in the legislative comprise at least a third of the council's membership. In 1943 Democratic strength in one house of the Kansas legislature dropped to less than 10 per cent of the membership, and it became impossible to obtain the required number of Democratic council members. The law was therefore changed to provide that party representation "shall be in proportion generally to the legislative number of members of the two major political parties in each house."[9]

The Kansas council was created at a trying time. Its survival attests to the service it quickly began rendering the Kansas legislature. The council and its staff, consisting of Dr. Guild and Camden Strain, helped prepare twenty-seven pieces of legislation for a special session early in 1934. By the 1935 legislative session studies had been made of 42 individual legislative policy items,[10] although the council's research department was not in full operation until August, 1934.[11] In 1936 it produced a series of distinguished studies of the social security program which was bursting upon the states.[12]

The status of the organization was enhanced as legislators came to realize the high regard in which it was held outside Kansas. One conscientious representative

noted for his dour attitude toward the council was im-
pressed when his request to the Council of State Governments for "the best available publication" on a specific
problem produced a copy of one of the Kansas council's
studies. After only a few years the term "Little Legislature," which had been attached with somewhat ambivalent meaning to the council soon after its creation, came
to be an accepted appellation.

The organization and operations of the Kansas council developed rather simply and with few major innovations into their present form.

> At first organized, the council . . . met in the
> senate chamber and followed the usual legisla-
> tive procedure even to three readings of propo-
> sals. In June of 1935, the rules were revised
> to eliminate much of the legislative formality.[13]

One other change, more gradually adopted over the
years, concerned the method by which the council's research department presents its findings to the council,
the legislature and the public. Initially this was in the
form of research reports—often bulky, ponderous, highly technical documents. The tendency in recent years
has been to limit the number of publications of this sort
to the barest minimum. Research is not wrapped up in
bound volumes. Much of it is submitted in the form of
memoranda, tabulations and other working papers in the
course of the work of council committees. The significance of this development is noted below.

Organization and Operation of the
Kansas Legislative Council

Organization

The basic structure consists of two distinct but
closely-knit elements: the legislative council proper,
which amounts to a permanent joint standing committee
of the legislature, and the research department.[14] The
council is made up of twenty-five members of the legislature plus two ex-officio members, the lieutenant–governor and the speaker of the house. The lieutenant–governor serves as chairman; the speaker is vice-
chairman. In addition, the state revisor of statutes is
ex-officio secretary of the legislative council, his function being essentially that of recorder.

The council contains no lay members or direct representatives of the executive branch of the Kansas government. The twenty-five legislative members are
appointed by the presiding officers of their respective
houses, subject to confirmation by the individual chambers. Ten members are chosen from the senate and
fifteen from the house. Through the 1945 legislative
session council appointments were made and announced
during the final week of the session. Beginning in 1947
the time was switched to the final day of the session,
as something of a protective move. By the mid-'40's,
the council had become sufficiently popular among the
legislators to produce some jockeying for membership
and occasional efforts to harass the council during the
closing days of the session by some disgruntled legislators who had vainly sought appointments. Hence the
change, which in the opinion of Dr. Guild has not been
a matter of great consequence. Inadvertent failure to
appoint the new council the mad hours of a sixty-day
biennial session has never occurred.[15]

Council appointments are for two years, extending
to the beginning of the session two years following the
appointments. The council does not function officially
during legislative session.

The research staff consists of a director, assistant
director, about six research associates and research
assistants, a fiscal officer, and a group of clerks. As
needed, the council research department makes use of
consultants. The revisor of statutes and his staff participate in the work of the research department insofar
as the drafting of bills and similar matters are involved.

The council received a biennial appropriation of
$ 10,000 for meetings and related matters beginning in
1933, but the research department was supported solely
by the Spelman Fund until June 30, 1937, with grants
totalling $ 35,000.[16] Currently the work of the Kansas
council is supported by appropriations well in excess of
$ 100,000 per year, including special appropriation items
earmarked for the support of individual studies.[17] The
council's financing usually includes a base-line appropriation to support a continuing level of activity plus
additional sums for large studies involving major increases in outlay.

In addition to the research staff there is another
group of employees under the jurisdiction of the council proper, selected by the council secretary (revisor
of statutes) subject to approval by a council committee.
This consists of at least two journal clerks, a few stenog-
raphers, a clerk, janitor, and one or two bill draftsmen. The work of these individuals is directly related
to the conduct of legislative sessions or the work of
the council proper, and is distinct from that of the research department, whose employees are selected by
its director subject to approval of the council's committee on budget and procedure.

The following chart showing in general outline the

ORGANIZATION OF RESEARCH DEPARTMENT, KANSAS LEGISLATIVE COUNCIL

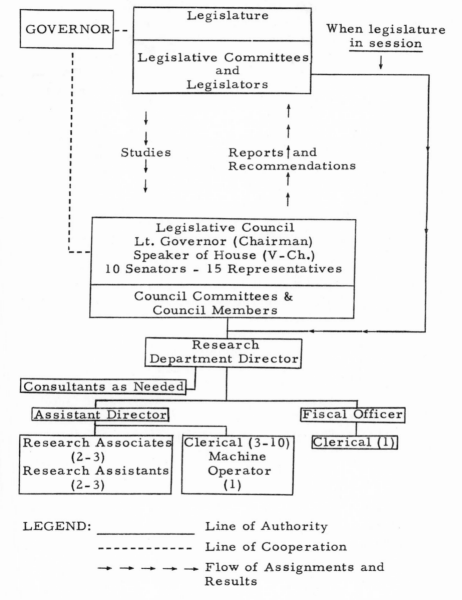

organization of the Kansas council helps explain its
structure. It does not furnish a great deal of insight into the heart of the council's operating process, which is
built around the work of the council's committees and
their relations with the research staff. It is in the committees that the council does its spadework, in a manner
somewhat similar to the standing committees of the
legislature itself. And it is the manner in which these
council committees function in relation to the research
department which distinguishes the council from the
legislative reference or research organization.

The popularity of the council has, of course, contributed to the effectiveness of its committee operations,
and to the maintenance of rather high standards of performance by the legislators who make up the council.
At least one previous term of service as a legislator is
customarily required as a qualification for appointment
to the council. "There are always two to three times
as many individual legislators wanting seats on the
council as are appointed."[18]   At one time, a balanced
pattern of geographical representation on the council
was stressed in making appointments, but emphasis'upon this requirement for selection has diminished considerably in recent years.

The Kansas council has the following ten standing
committees, each composed of five members, two from
the Senate and three from the House:[19]

    Agriculture and Livestock
    Assessment and Taxation
    Charitable and Benevolent Institutions
    Education
    Federal, State and Local Government
    Judiciary
    Labor and Industries
    Legislative Budget
    Public Welfare
    Roads and Highways

Each council member serves on two committees, permitting a total of fifty committee assignments. In addition, the council has three "operational committees": Committee on Committees, composed of the chairman, vice-chairman, and five other members, two from the Senate and three from the House, which makes appointments to the council's standing committees; a Calendar Committee responsible for determining the order of business, and a Committee on Rules, Procedure, and Budget, with five members divided between Senate and House in the customary two and three fashion. This last committee reviews the council's budget, supervises the general administration of the council's research department, and passes upon suggestions for council projects which are not submitted in the form of proposals from the legislature itself.[20]

Finally, there is a legislative steering committee, appointed by the Committee on Committees prior to each legislative session. Consisting of five members, its task is to "present to the appropriate committees of the legislature the proposals, bills and other recommendations submitted by the Council to the legislature and follow the same through the legislature and see that they receive a fair presentation before the committees."[21]

The Council Process

The essential function of the Kansas council is the analysis and evaluation of matters prior to legislative consideration. The council's mandate is broad. The 1933 statue authorized it to:

1. Collect information concerning the governmental and general welfare of the state.

2. Examine the effects of previously enacted statutes and recommend amendments thereto.

3. Deal with important issues of public policy and questions of state-wide interest.

4. Investigate and study the possibilities for consolidations in the state government, for elimination of all unnecessary activities and of all duplication in office personnel and equipment, for the coordination of departmental activities, and for methods of increasing efficiency and of effecting economies.

5. Investigate and study the possibilities of reforming the system of local government with a view of simplifying the organization of government.

6. Cooperate with the administration in devising means of enforcing the laws and improving the effectiveness of administrative methods.

7. Present to the next legislature a legislative program in the form of bills or otherwise.

The only formal coercive power possessed by the council is the authority to obtain information through its committees and research staff. Subpoenas may be issued and witnesses may be compelled to appear and produce documents. The subpoena power has never been used, although its presence was sufficient in one instance to produce testimony from a witness who might otherwise have been unavailable. The ultimate authority of the council has through its entire history rested upon its status, its processes and its product, rather than the use of coercion.

In outline, the council process is quite simple, consisting of the initiation and study of proposals, and the formulation of recommendations for transmittal to the legislature.

1. Proposals for council study. Council assignments may be initiated in only two ways: by a concurrent legislative resolution, or by the presentation of a proposal to the council by a member of the legislature.[22] In practice, council studies are initiated by formal

legislative action or proposals made by members of the council, rather than other legislators. Individual legislators are free to submit proposals, and interest groups are welcome to call upon the council to undertake studies. The council, however, retains control over the scope and content of its efforts excepting those assigned by the entire legislature. All proposals emanating from individuals or groups must be presented in writing by a member of the legislature, in a prescribed form.[23] The sponsor may, if he wishes, explain and discuss his proposal to the full council at a regular meeting. It may be accepted or rejected by the council or referred to committee for further consideration.

Two-thirds to three-fourths of the council's assignments during a given biennium stem from individual proposals rather than legislative resolution.[24] And most of these are made by members of the council. Some stem from recommendations contained in the governor's message; others may originate in the interests of individual council members, in suggestions to them from outside sources, or out of earlier council committee undertakings. Executive departments of Kansas state government not infrequently suggest council studies of problems or developments affecting their operations.[25] The following table summarizes the sources of council proposals over an 11-year period, 1933-44.

Although legislative assignments naturally receive top priority, the council's resources are adequate to permit it to cope with a variety of additional tasks. One attractive consequence of its procedure for initiating projects is the ability to begin studies at almost any time during the period between legislative sessions. The last proposal adopted by the council between the 1953 and 1955 sessions was approved in May, 1954, only seven months before the next legislative session.

"All our studies are controversial." The Kansas

TABLE 3

SOURCE OF KANSAS LEGISLATIVE COUNCIL PROPOSALS

Introduced By	Number of Proposals					
	1933-1934	1935-1936	1937-1938	1939-1940	1941-1942	1943-1944
Submitted by Legislature	0	0	3c	7	9	17
Council Members	89	8	33	29	10d	19
Council Committees	5	4	0	8	5d	10d
Other Members of Legislature	0	1	5	9	3	0
TOTAL	94a	13b	41	53	27e	46

a. At least 33 proposals resulted directly or indirectly from messages of the governor to the council:
2 in the first session, 21 in the second session called to prepare for the special session of the legislature,
and 10 in later sessions. Six other proposals arose from communications from private individuals or groups.

b. Much of the most important work of the council in 1935-36 was done without the introduction and approval of
formal proposals, for instance, unemployment compensation, social security, loan sharks, homestead exemption.
Some are represented by council motions and communications received. One proposal was introduced by a
member following a communication from the governor.

c. Although proposals 37, 38, and 39 were introduced by a council committee, they arose directly from House
Resolution No. 16 of the Special Session of 1938.

d. 1941-42. Members - One followed recommendation of Governor; Committees, at least three arose from answers
to survey of needed war legislation, and one from a group appearance before the council.
1943-44. One of these proposals was suggested by a communication from the Governor; one by a communication
from a Senator not on the council, and five by communications from private citizens or groups.

e. In addition, two resolutions for investigations, No. 3 on social welfare audit contracts and No. 5 on labor unions
were the occasion for extensive council activity.

council does not operate on the fringes of the legislative process. A review of the subjects under study at any one time practically amounts to an itemization of major pending legislative issues. For example, at its May, 1954, meeting, the council had under consideration a group of more than forty proposals, including these:[26]

> The adequacy of current standards of teacher certification.
> A study of problems under the law of water appropriation.
> The need for licensing insurance agents.
> The regulation of lobbying.
> The regulation of small loans.
> The desirability of a "right-to-work" law.
> Standardizing medical care of welfare clients.
> The adequacy of boarding and nursing home licensing arrangements.
> The need for a possible reorganization of state and local public health services.
> A proposal for compulsory periodic vehicle inspection.
> Highway user taxation—the question of ton-mile v. supplemental fuel taxes for trucks.

The list is only illustrative; a review of a series of the progress reports issued quarterly by the Kansas council gives impressive testimony to the diversity of its studies. "The council, by its present methods, does cover practically all of the important state-wide items which come before the legislature."[27]

The ability of the council to tackle issues is further evidenced by the fact that no interim legislative committees have been created in Kansas since 1935; "studies which were in the past assigned to special committees are now cleared through the council."[28]

The scope of the council's work is, of course, a

two-sided coin. A natural tendency toward legislative buck-passing has occasionally been reflected in assignments made to the council over the years.

> There has been a continued tendency on the part of the legislature to "pass the buck" by using reference for study by the council as a method of postponing action. In other words, the study may have been directed not because the current legislature was sure that the succeeding legislature would insist upon having the material because it wanted to pass a law on the subject, but merely to enable the current legislature to get rid of the subject. We had numerous instances of this in the earlier years, and the legislative council members did not like the situation.
>
> More recently the rules have made it increasingly difficult to instruct the legislative council to make studies. With our bicameral system, it now requires a Concurrent Resolution to direct a council study. In the earlier years such direction came from a simple Senate or House Resolution. Now the resolutions are referred to committees in both houses and then given careful scrutiny, with the result, for example, that several of the proposals introduced in 1951 were not passed.
>
> May I say first that we have no such "pass the buck" instructions in the nine concurrent resolutions adopted this year. Only one such resolution was passed two years ago. . . . In 1947 there were two resolutions for studies which some people thought were of this character. . . . In general there is now definite resistance to attempts to use the legislative council as an alibi.[29]

2. The Council's Study Procedure. In the council committees the yeoman work of the council takes place; some of this work is exceedingly complex, at times dull,

at others highly controversial, and often difficult and
unglamorous. All proposals are assigned for study to
one or another of the council's committees. At any
given time a committee may have eight or more individual studies under consideration.

A study usually involves a combination of the efforts
of committee members and one or more members of
the research staff. The handling of a given topic is determined by its nature. At one end of a scale are occasional subjects which are almost entirely matters of
political determination; at the other are highly technical
questions in which there may be little or no public interest at the time.

In approaching its assignments a committee may
use some or all of the following procedures: research
memoranda and reports prepared by the staff, public
hearings on specific proposals or issues, and "informational conferences," designed to sound out interest
groups or to shape interest in some issue under study.

The customary first step in the handling of an assignment is the preparation by the research department of
a background report. Not uncommonly a council committee will outline its initial needs or desires to the research department at a committee meeting during the
quarterly council meeting at which the proposal was introduced.

> The research department, under such instruc-
> tions, may prepare a formal report to be sub-
> mitted to the committee, and, later to be dupli-
> cated for distribution to the members of the
> legislature and to a mailing list of 1,000 citizens.
> Frequently, however the research department
> sends out to members of the committee, as
> soon as any material is in sufficient shape, a
> report of progress, which may run from one
> typewritten page to thirty or forty.[30]

As many as 200-250 such memoranda may be prepared
in the course of a biennium.

   Working by correspondence and in regular or special meetings, the committee shapes its study, perhaps
over a period of months or even a couple of years. The
process involves a subtle and complicated meshing of
staff research and political evaluation. On one hand,
"objectivity is the watchword of the council research
staff."[31]   On the other, "all our studies are controversial." "The main point is that of divòrcing the objective
research activity from the debate on policy," according
to the research director. Yet the divorce is not so significant as the wedding—the linking of "objective research activity" with political judgment and policy positions.

   This synthesis is what Sam Wilson had in mind
when he first conceived of the legislative council. It is
a delicate thing. One can, for example, build a rather
convincing case to the effect that facts and values cannot be separated in the manner required by this procedure. In any event, council-type organization is always subject to stress and tension upon this point. The
effectiveness and success of the Kansas council requires
the maintenance of an aura of impartiality insofar as research is concerned. The inevitable and partially uncon-
scious tendency of research workers to impose judgments, to submit opinions in one form or another, to
become party to the issues themselves, must be constantly guarded against.

   In an intimate and informal interview lasting over
two days, one sensed the fact that this need for neutrality
is never out of the thoughts of the man who has directed
the research of the Kansas council for a quarter—century. It is reflected in the staffing of the research department, in the careful scrutiny of reports before they
are distributed, and in the complete absence of publicity-

seeking by the research department and its members.
An effective myth of objectivity has been established in
the Kansas council; this has been the sine qua non of the
organization's research procedure.

The essential synthesis of technical knowledge and
political judgment sometimes involves more than the
joint efforts of a council committee and the research
staff. The council members themselves do not serve as
the sole spokesmen for political interests. Council committees at times function as sounding boards for interest groups, as investigative bodies, and upon occasion
as media for stimulating the growth of public interest in
some matter under consideration. "Procedure . . . cannot be a routine thing. Much depends upon the particular
nature of the topics."[32] Whether a council committee
will use hearings or the technique described as "informational conferences" is determined by the nature of the
particular undertaking. The full council must approve
proposals for such hearings or conferences.[33]

In the Kansas council the importance of informational conferences as a method of building or evaluating
public opinion has been stressed. The differences between an informational conference and a hearing consist
of the relative informality of the conference and the
more general or tentative nature of the subjects under
consideration. Council hearings are conducted on a
systematic basis. A transcript is taken (although not
necessarily transcribed) of testimony received; in addition, time for testimony is allocated on a fifty-fifty
basis between opposing sides being heard on a given
issue.[34]

The Kansas Legislative Council meets regularly
four times a year. Its quarterly meetings, provided
for by the rules governing its operation, normally occur
in March, May, September, and November. They last
at least two days, and normally begin at 10:00 in the

morning. The council committees also meet either before or after the formal council meeting, in order to
save time and travel expense. Under the rules governing the council's operation, "a committee shall report
on all matters referred to it not later than the next
quarterly meeting of the Council."[35] This arrangement
makes it difficult for a committee assignment to be deliberately or inadvertently buried (a rather marked contrast to the procedure of legislative standing committees.). Meetings prior to a legislative session in
September and November often last three or four days.
They include a rather hectic combination of committee
sessions and deliberations of the full council.

Under the Kansas arrangement for combining research and policy judgements, each member of the council's professional staff works on a continuing basis with
one or more individual committees. It would be humanly
impossible for the director to attempt to serve the entire
committee structure. As a result, a great deal of responsibility devolves upon each member of the small,
able research staff.[36]

The Legislative Program

"The fundamental purpose in the creation of a legislative council is the preparation of a program for the
next legislative session."[37]

The program of the Kansas Council is the product
of the efforts of its committees, as these are screened
by the council. It is not a program in the sense of a
full agenda intended to encompass the whole scope of
legislative consideration. It is, in other words, "open-
ended," and consists of the product of the council's
work on perhaps forty or fifty subjects. The legislature
is likely to take up a considerable number of other

matters, but over the years the subjects of council study have constituted nearly all of the major issues before the Kansas legislature.

The council's program is not presented in the form of recommendations for legislative ratification; it consists of "recommendations for consideration by the legislature."[38] At every possible opportunity the director and the council members are inclined to stress this matter very heavily, drawing an emphatic distinction between "recommendations for consideration," and "recommendations for action."

Prior to each legislative session the council prepares and submits a report with recommendations, representing the formal conclusion of its anticipatory efforts.[39] Many of the recommendations are stated in the form of bills prefaced by explanatory summaries of the council study and conclusions. Other recommendations may not be in the form of proposed legislation, and at times the recommendation of the council may be merely to the effect that in its judgment no action is necessary.

All council committee recommendations are reviewed carefully at regular meetings of the full council, which decides whether recommendations are to be submitted in the form of proposed legislation.[40]

The final council decisions and its legislative report are prefaced by a systematic communications procedure. The entire council is briefed at least quarterly on the work of each of its committees. Following each quarterly council meeting the council staff prepares a progress report summarizing the status of each project under consideration. This is distributed to each member of the legislature, as well as to a non-legislative mailing list of several hundred people. Research reports and formal memoranda are distributed to the entire legislature, although working papers prepared for individual committees are commonly distributed only to the committee concerned. Official reports of the council and major research reports are distributed to libraries in and out of Kansas, to constituents as requested by individual legislators and to approximately twenty-two hundred organizations and individuals. As a result, members of the legislature have at least had an opportunity for a fairly thorough briefing on each of the issues to be submitted by the council for consideration. Immediately following the elections preceding a legislative session a careful effort is made to brief new members of the legislature. They receive copies of the council's reports and their requests for further information are solicited by mail.

During the legislative session the council per se is dormant except for its steering committee. This committee serves as the formal link between the council and the legislature during the session. Prior to 1943, bills recommended by the council were "parcelled out by members of the council who were returning to the legislature."[41] Since 1943 council bills have been referred by the council to the appropriate standing committees in the Senate and House for such disposition as these committees determine. The bills appear as committee bills introduced by the regular standing committees, although it is generally known that they are bills upon which the council has worked.[42] Responsibility for them rests, however, with the standing committees.

The council steering committee, created in 1945, has this specific assignment: "To follow the legislative council bills through the legislature and see that they receive a fair presentation before the committees."[43] This system appears to have worked successfully. Under the guidance of the steering committee, council members make personal presentations before the appropriate standing committees, explaining the background of each proposal. The tone of this process appears to be one of advising and explaining rather than aggressive sponsorship or advocacy. So far as one can judge, the demeanor of the council steering committee and the individual council members has not created any significant resentment within the legislature.

The work of the steering committee represents the final link in a process whose essential characteristic is integration of one sort or another. It completes the gearing the council's efforts to those of the full legislative assembly. Thus the products of one or two years of continuing study become embedded in the legislative process, and in such a manner as to avoid—in Kansas at any rate—a feeling on the part of the legislature that it has been superseded.

An Evaluation

The Kansas Legislative Council epitomizes the concept of the legislative program planning council. The Kansas Council is something of an "ideal type."

The Council and the Legislature

"The council idea is based on using legislators without any attempt to metamorphose them over night into a brain thrust or guiding angels free from behavior normal to legislators."[44] The Kansas Legislative Council is of, by, and for the legislature. It contains no representation from other branches of state government. Its work is not inherently incompatible with the character of legislature and the legislators—although participation in the council does place a considerable burden upon each individual council member.

One of the most significant aspects of the relationship of the council to the full legislative assembly is expressed in the following passage:

> Two factors enable them (the legislators) to function as they could not during the regular session. The first is the quarterly meeting, with freedom from rush and pressure; no necessity for immediate decision, concentration on fundamentals instead of upon details, language of bills; opportunity to talk all subjects over for three months at home before returning; and time for further considerations spread over two years. There are no special local bills to push through. Log rolling is gone. Nothing remains but major state problems. Second, there is the research staff, to do most of the detailed work for committees and members, to supplement with additional information at the next meeting, and ultimately to report to the legislature such additional information as the council may direct.
>
> The council member nevertheless remains strictly a legislator. Many members will probably run for re-election or for another office. They are naturally contemplating the next campaign. They must also think in terms of their membership on regular committees, of the give-and-take which will normally result in the regular session. In consequence, legislators have definite limitations in planning a program to extend beyond two years. They are particularly fitted, however, to guage accurately the program which will best meet the needs of the next session. In so doing, they do not sit down to plan such a program deliberately. A few items are selected as the result of conscious effort. Many others are chosen in response to the very same stimuli to which legislators have always reacted.[45]

In a sense, the council consists of a selected seg-
ment of the legislature, functioning legislatively, but
free from the pressures and disruptions which always
disturb and sometimes seem to dominate American
state legislative sessions. The work of the legislative
council amounts to a highly <u>focused</u> legislative process.
It preserves the concept of the "citizen legislator"—
that amateur, representative individual who, by the very
nature of his amateurism remains close to the people
and the groups for whom he speaks. Dedication to this
idea of the amateur (or at least part-time) legislator is
a high-universal phenomenon at the state level of American government. It sets one of the boundaries within
which an entity such as a legislative council must function if it is to be effective. The compatibility of the
council idea as represented in Kansas with this inclination toward the non-professional legislator is a very
potent asset.

One characteristic of the Kansas council is its
"openness." The idea has two aspects: In the first
place, the work of the Kansas council is not done behind locked doors. Deliberate and effective efforts are
made to the contrary. Members of the legislature as
well as interested segments of the public have every
basis for feeling that they know what goes on in the
council during the interim period between legislative
sessions.

In another sense, too, the Kansas council is an
"open" organization. A sizeable majority of proposals
for council studies are formally initiated by its own
members, but this fact is quite misleading. The council members respond "to the very same stimuli to
which legislators have always reacted." They maintain no monopoly on the determination of subjects to be
taken up for study; rather they serve as a group of
respondors to expressed interests and felt needs. A

direct channel to the entire council is open to any member of the Kansas State Legislature, but in practice the informal suggestions of legislators and constituent groups usually lead to the preparation of formal proposals by individual council members.

The size of the Kansas Legislative Council, with its total of twenty-seven members—including the presiding officers of the two houses—is of more than mechanical significance. It provides for continuity in the operations and orientation of the council. It is generally safe to assume that half the members of a given Kansas Legislative Council will be serving in the legislature at the session following their period of council service. Each council goes out of business with the start of the legislative session following its creation and there is no inherent assurance that an individual member will be reappointed, but the fact of a sizeable body insures a degree of continuity. Such has always been the case; and this enables the maintenance of a tradition of operation established during the first years of the Kansas council's experience.

Finally, the size of the Kansas council has insured a healthy diversity. At no time has the council been seriously accused of not being representative in the sense that some major interest was not adequately accounted for by the makeup of the council itself. Disappearance of an early concern with the need for geographical representation on the council suggests that problems of representation are not felt to exist.

The general caliber of the members of the Kansas council over the years merits consideration. In Kansas one must be an experienced legislator to be eligible for council membership. A council appointment is not a political plum. Real work is involved, and the remuneration of $ 12.00 per day plus seven cents per mile for travel is hardly sufficient to attract profit-seekers.[46]

To continue in good standing as a member of the Kansas
council, one must carry his fair share of the load. The
ultimate sanction consists of a request for resignation;
it has seldom been used. Willingness to work is a pre-
requisite for appointment to the council, and a rather
delicate and thorough process of screening takes place
during a legislative session prior to the appointment of
a new council. It seems likely that Dr. Guild is consulted in connection with contemplated council appointments.

Relationships between council membership and
membership on legislative standing committees are
relatively unstructured. There is no persistent corre-
lation between the two. Legislative leaders usually
serve on the council, but this is a result of the general
selection process rather than any deliberate arrangements for the appointment of particular committee
chairmen to the council. The intentional openness of
this relationship between council and legislature is
based upon these considerations:

1. The aim of maintaining a sense of distinction
between the council and the legislature. The council
proposes: the legislature disposes. A systematic fabric of relationships between council and standing committees might be viewed as intended to foster the approval of council proposals. The council's steering
committee is the only body whose purpose is to follow
up council recommendations. Partly it is because this
committee is an identifiable entity that it has avoided
the appearance of going beyond its avowed objective of
seeing that council proposals are not lost in the legislative shuffle.

2. The council comes into being after the legislative session rather than before it. The relative break
in the continuity of council operations comes at the beginning of a biennial legislative session. It is possible

to select council members in terms of their committee work during the session just past, but there is no inherent assurance that these same persons will be members of chairmen of particular committees in the session following the council's activity.

3.   The factors influencing the selection of members of the legislative council are not entirely those which tend to determine standing committee assignments. In choosing council members such criteria are applied as minority party representation, and perhaps the interest of particular individuals in anticipated subjects of council study.

The adjectives which appear to best describe the general tone of relations between the Kansas council and the Kansas legislature would seem to be these: "confidence, respect, lack of distrust." Kansans proudly refer to their legislative council as "the Little Legislature."[47] The term is one of fondness rather than resentment.

Fundamentally, the function of the Kansas council in relation to the legislature is preparatory. It is a matter of sorting, organizing, analyzing, and focusing— a process somewhat analogous to the pre-digestion of food to prepare it for a stomach not fully capable of handling it in its original form.

It is not incorrect to visualize the council as a "leadership process," although the council is somewhat hard to picture in terms of traditional concepts of leadership centering around some tangible authority-symbol. In truth, however, democratic leadership is a process of direction-setting and adaptation operating in a context of acceptance and shared objectives.[48] The significance of the council does not rest on the fact that it furnishes a valuable research product. The research function is an integral element, but its importance lies in the way in which it is deliberately and effectively

subordinated. It is the dual linking of technical research with political judgment and of the council operation with the legislature in session that is significant.
Democratic leadership has been described as the functioning of "a catalyst which speeded up the natural processes of the group and helped it to attain the structure
which was the most suitable one in the circumstances."[49]
This idea of a catalytic function is certainly applicable
to the Kansas council—as is the idea of the Kansas
legislature as a relatively cohesive group.

The form of the Kansas council process is singularly well tailored to its environment—so well that it
is hardly evident. "The great rulers—the people do not
notice their existence."[50] The persistent, effective,
adaptable leadership of the council is in a sense un-
noticed, as a result of the manner in which the council
process is subordinated to the functioning of the legislature in session. The fundamental contribution of the
council is to the process of arriving at policy decisions
in the Kansas legislature, through the preliminary or-
dering and analysis of the major objects of the legislative process.

The Council and the Governor

The Kansas Legislative Council vividly reflects the
American concept of separation of powers. The council is founded upon the idea of legislative independence
of the executive.

"Governors have generally desired to be consulted
regarding appointments to the Kansas Legislative Council, but this does not necessarily occur."[51] Gubernatorial influence over appointments to the Kansas council
is an occasional consequence of a governor's relationships with legislative leaders. Generally, the

composition of the Kansas council has not been significantly influenced over the years by the desires or actions of Kansas governors. More important, the functioning of the council has not been impeded or thwarted
by the exercise of gubernatorial power.

> The governors themselves have always been
> very favorable to the development of the Legis-
> lative Council. Governor Landon (1933-36) ex-
> pressed himself publicly and positively in
> favor of the agency. Governor Huxman (1937-
> 38), a Democratic governor, with a Republican
> Legislature, was non-committal, although im-
> portant Democratic officials under him were
> strongly in support of the Council. Governor
> Ratner (1939-42) was strongly favorable, part
> of his statements to that effect being in his
> official messages to the Legislative Council
> in those years. Governor Schoeppel (1943-
> 46) is working very closely with the Legisla-
> tive Council and believes strongly in the pro-
> cedure.[52]

The definite separation between the council and the
executive branch by no means amounts to a complete
breach. The council research staff works confidentially
and informally for the incoming governor following his
election, briefing him on pending problems and forthcoming issues.[53] The content of the governor's message to his first session of the Kansas legislature usually reflects the results of this assistance. In general,
however, "there are no formal working relations between the governor and the council or the council's research staff."[54]
The research department of the Kansas council is
perhaps the best informed center of information on
Kansas government and its problems and needs. This
is one reason for the customary tender of assistance
to an incoming governor made by the director of the

research department, usually through the governor's secretary.[55] When the governor takes office on the eve of a legislative session the Kansas council has completed its work on a series of proposals to be submitted to the legislature. Invariably these include issues upon which the governor has campaigned, or regarding which he is likely to have commitments. In the interests of both courtesy and coordination, the governor is briefed concerning the impending council program.

To sum up, relationship between governor and council rests at best upon a reorganized mutuality of interests and the accepted independence of the legislature. At no time has the Kansas council suffered from staunch, effective gubernatorial opposition.[56] The council has not radically altered the position of the governor in Kansas by usurping his potential position of leadership; his power over the legislature has traditionally been quite limited. Undoubtedly, the council helps define the limits within which gubernatorial leadership of the legislature may be effective, in the sense that council studies and council conclusions tend to define the terms of issues.

The Council and the Administrative Branch

> The strongest administrative support has
> come from the various boards and commissions with which the Research Department
> has worked in connection with its numerous
> studies for the Legislative Council.[57]

The statement suggests the generally satisfactory relations which exist between the council and administrative agencies. The council is a combination of advisor and overseer, management studies staff, legislative liaison unit, and budget review agency. Council-agency relations reflect the character of the

Kansas governmental-political setting, including the relatively limited power of the governor.

The council is not primarily an investigative agency, but it does serve as a legislative watchdog, having had a striking success in conducting certain investigations of administrative agencies soon after it was founded. Within the council staff one finds a certain pride in its role of helping keep the administrative agencies of Kansas honest. Not a lot of trouble has been encountered in this work, however, and there appears to be no strong overt resentment of the council's efforts in this field; these have been marked by a happy combination of fairness and competence.

The council and its research department have undertaken a number of organization studies — of the Board of Social Welfare, of institutional management in Kansas state government, of financial administration, personnel administration, highway organization, and various administrative procedures. The research department

> is frequently called in to discuss methods
> which may be employed by new departments,
> particularly. In addition, the fiscal methods
> or systems of reporting expenditures and
> budget requests have been under concen-
> trated study the past several years, gen-
> erally with emphasis shifting from one
> department to another.[58]

Not unwisely, heads of various departments of Kansas state government tend to consult the head of the council's research department about proposals and recommendations they are considering. The council research department "checks and verifies for legislative committees reports or studies made by administrative departments."[59] It also assists in legislative consideration of the Kansas budget.

Thus the council and its research department serve as a combined planning-advisory-and-control unit. The council possesses no direct supervisory authority, but it does have extensive powers of review and a great degree of influence. The Council, concerned with efficiency, economy and program needs rather than with a Watch and Ward Society approach, walks comfortably in that no-man's land of administrative agency-legislature relations. By its rather firm grasp of agency plans and activities it helps avoid the all-too-common legislative suspicion of the presumably dubious and mysterious aims of the administrative branch. As an aid to the avoidance of trouble and a channel for reaching the legislature, the council is accepted and perhaps even welcomed by Kansas state administrative agencies.

The Council and Interest Groups

In the earliest days of its operation the research department of the Kansas council clashed with a powerful Kansas lobbyist who questioned the honesty and accuracy of certain research findings. In a dramatic show-down the accuracy of the council report was proved and a thoroughly beaten lobbyist was forced to admit the error of his ways.[60]

This experience helped establish a pattern of relations with lobbyists and other representatives of interest groups within the state. On one hand, it is generally known that irresponsible assertions are likely to be exposed. On the other, the council takes no general position regarding the activities of interest groups, but encourages them to submit proposals for council study and in general seeks to maintain amicable relationships. The council itself is after all a product of the efforts of one of them.

The Council and the Parties

Dr. Guild has described the Kansas council as a "bipartisan thing,"[61] and the council itself has not been adversely effected by the workings of partisan politics. A strict "hands off" policy has always been maintained toward the research staff; partisanism has not entered into the selection, retention or promotion of research staff members. At the same time, the assertion of partisan positions in the deliberations of the council is quite compatible with the nature of that body. Finally, the whole process of policy making in Kansas as in many other states is not constantly dominated by partisanism; legislative issues are not primarily matters of partisan politics.[62]

The Test of Results

The Kansas Legislative Council does produce results. But what results? And how are they to be evaluated?

The general tendency in examining any legislative council appears to be to look at its "batting average," or to compare the number of recommendations made with the number adopted. This can be both misleading and undesirable, although it has a certain utility. A consistent record over the years of recommendations ignored would be a good basis for questioning and effectiveness of the organization. On the other hand, a persistently high batting average might suggest that the council is superseding the legislature. The continued unquestioning adoption of council proposals is not entirely compatible with the concept of "recommendations for consideration" under which the Kansas council purports to operate.

The culmination of the council process in Kansas is in its recommendations:

The general practice of making recommendations means that the subcommittees working on
each subject must go much more thoroughly
into the subject if they are going to come out
with specific recommendations. The member of a committee who must make up his
mind what recommendations he will stand for,
of necessity, must comprehend the research
material much more fully than will the member who is not required to make a recommendation. In other words, council committees
become much better directors of research,
seeking answers to the question in their
minds in order to make recommendations
to the council as to what the council should
recommend to the legislature. This is by
far the most important aspect of this entire debate about recommending.[63]

"In the earlier days the Kansas council's recommendations accepted ran as low as twenty-six per cent
to twenty-nine per cent for bills passed."[64] By the mid-
1940's, however, as many as seventy per cent of the
bills recommended by the council were being adopted
by the legislature in one form or another. An even
higher percentage came out of committee or passed one
house only. Approximately the same percentages applied to recommendations not accompanied by bills. In
1951 about sixty-six per cent of council bill recommendations were enacted.[65] Practically 100 per cent of the
council's recommendations that no action be taken have
been consistently accepted over more than a decade.[66]
     In commenting upon these statistics, Dr. Guild ex-
pressed the opinion that the adoption of seventy per cent
of the bills recommended by the council was probably
undesirable: a high percentage of adoptions may mean
that a council has had it "too many minor proposals, not
of a controversial nature." The only plausible alternative conclusions would be one of uncritical legislative

acceptance or a striking ability of the council to anticipate the decisions of the full legislature.

More important than batting averages as a basis
for evaluation is the test of actual legislative consideration. On this score, the record of the Kansas council is
excellent. Practically none of the council's proposals,
whether in bill form or not, die in committee without
having at least received specific attention.[67]

The following illustration of the difficulty of any effort to apply a statistical test of effectiveness to a legislative council supports the assertion that the best test
of council effectiveness is legislative consideration:

> Several years back we had an important drain-
> age control bill which was highly controversial.
> It passed both houses, with important amend-
> ments of the second house, and consequently
> went through five conference committees be-
> fore an agreement was reached. The fifth
> conference committee report reached the
> floor at two-thirty a.m. on the last night
> of the session and failed to be adopted by
> two votes. Now was council successful or
> not successful in its study of the drainage
> problem? The bill failed to pass, true,
> but it was a main bone of contention through-
> out the session and passed both houses. If
> approval means final passage, then the legis-
> lature disapproved the council's work since
> the bill did not become law. If approval means
> that the legislature made continuous use of
> the council's study and recommendations
> throughout the session on a heavily contro-
> versial matter, then the legislative council
> was very successful in preparing that par-
> ticular job for the legislative session.
>
> In general, I think we should say that the
> legislature now makes very excellent use
> of the council studies.[68]

Other factors also pertain to an effort to assess the effectiveness of the legislative council. The existence of that agency has helped reduce the workload of the Kansas legislature. This reduction has not been so significant in terms of sheer numbers of bills as in the elimination of "many of the former bills of a freak-type."

> What does seem particularly significant is the reduction in the number of bills introduced in the last three days before the deadline for introduction of member bills, which comes about the middle of February. Since the council has covered the general program pretty thoroughly, there seems to be less tendency on the part of the numbers to throw in hastily drafted bills merely on the supposition that they might want to have them in case certain aspects of the program were not covered.[69]

The Kansas council has had little effect on the log jam which characterizes the end of a legislative session. "We cannot see that the existence of the council has as yet changed the long established habits of the legislative session."[70]   At the same time, it seems that the number of significant matters which receive only cursory consideration as a result of the log jam has declined significantly, "but I doubt if this is susceptible of absolute proof."[71]

There remains one final test of the effectiveness of the Kansas council—survival. On this score the organization must certainly be rated highly. Research appropriations have grown steadily. There have been no threats to the council's existence in more than fifteen years. It would be difficult and probably deceptive to accumulate statistics on dollars saved in the administration of Kansas government as a consequence of the efforts of the Kansas Legislative Council, or to attempt to compare the "quality" of legislation on specific matters enacted in Kansas and elsewhere. Nonethe less, in the Kansas legislature, in the administrative branch of Kansas government, in the newspapers and political organizations of the state of Kansas, in the Council of State Governments, and in legislative service organizations throughout the United States, the Kansas council is highly regarded; and this regard appears clearly to stem from a recognition of the manner in which it fulfills its mandate.[72]

One final observation must become part of any assessment of the Kansas council. The relation of the form or structure of an organization to its success is essentially negative; a poorly designed process is less likely to succeed. On the other hand, good form or structure per se is no assurance of success. Certainly this is true in the case of the Kansas Legislative Council. One cannot evaluate the full significance of personality as a factor in its attainments other than to say that it must be very good indeed. The zeal and ability of its director have become legendary. The integrity and earnest striving for objectivity which characterize the research department can be more readily felt than described. These things are critical factors in the functioning of the Kansas council. They have a direct bearing on the question of its "transplantability." Efforts have been made to apply the Kansas council process to other settings. They have involved far more than copying a statute, a structure of organization, and a manual of procedure.

Notes

1. The following account is based upon interviews with Dr. Frederick H. Guild, director of the Kansas Council, and with Mr. Sam Wilson, retired, of Topeka, Kansas, on August 27, and 28, 1954.

2. Graves, State Government, op. cit., p. 260.

3. "Facts Concerning the Kansas Legislative Council," Memorandum, Research Department, Kansas Legislative Council, May 2, 1945, pp. 6-7. (Typewritten.)

4. Ibid.

5. Book of the States 1956-57, p. 123.

6. "Facts Concerning the Kansas Council," op. cit., p. 17.

7. Kansas' Experiment With a Legislative Council, Bulletin No. 42, Research Department, Kansas Legislative council, August, 1936, p. 6.

8. Kansas General Statutues Annotated, chapter 46, sections 301-312.

9. Kansas Laws, 1943, chapter 192.

10. F. H. Guild, "Accomplishments of the Kansas Legislative Council" (May 23, 1935), unpaged. (Mimeographed).

11. "Kansas Experiment," op. cit., p. 2.

12. "Legislative Councils, An Article and Bibliography," op. cit., lists these at pp. 11-12.

13. "Kansas Experiment," op. cit., p. 3.

14. The following description is based chiefly upon "Facts Concerning the Kansas Legislative Council," plus a collection of memoranda and papers from the files of the Kansas Council and notes from an interview with Dr. Frederick Guild.

15. Beginning in 1955, Kansas adopted the practice of annual legislative session; see The Book of the States 1956-57, p. 98.

16. It is difficult to furnish a better illustration of the role of the legislature in the initial establishment of the council than the fact that much of its initial financial support came not from the legislature, but to it from a private foundation.

17. Book of the States 1958-59, p. 70.

18. Guild interview.

19. "Forms, Rules and Committee Assignments of the 1953-54 Kansas Legislative Council," Prepared by Franklin Corrick, Secretary, Topeka, Kansas, June, 1953, pp. 9-10.

20. Ibid., p. 9.

21. Ibid., p. 10.

22. Ibid., p. 10.

23. Ibid., Rules 9-12.

24. According to Dr. Guild, during the 1953-54 biennium the council's workload consisted of 44 studies, 12 originating with the legislature and the others within the council.

25. "Administrative agencies tell us that they secure much more extended and favorable consideration from legislative council committees than is possible before committees of the regular session. While some of the reports on administrative work have not been favorable, the departments concerned have usually felt the procedure and findings were sympathetic and fair. . . . Some of these suggestions for studies actually arise in administrative offices which feel that a legislative study under the council system produces better findings and results than they could receive by an administrative study." "Facts," op. cit., p. 22.

26. "Progress Report, May Council Meeting," Kansas Legislative Council, Publication No. 191, May, 1954, 12 pp. (Multilithed.)

27. "Facts," op. cit., p. 9.

28. Ibid., p. 6.

29. Letter from F. H. Guild to Dr. Roger V. Shumate, Director, Nebraska Legislative Council, April 7, 1951.

30. "Facts," op. cit., p. 10.

31. Guild interview.

32. "Facts concerning the Kansas Legislative Council," op. cit., p. 12.

33. "Forms, Rules and Committee Assignments,"
op. cit., Rule 18, p. 11.

34. Guild interview.

35. Rule 14.

36. Guild interview. It is somewhat amusing to
note the absence of any women on the professional
staff of the Kansas Council's Research Department,
which is explained by the nature of the working relationships between the research personnel and the council
committees and the attitude of the director. Because of
the heavy responsibilities which inherently fall upon the
individual research worker, these persons must be precise, discrete and positive in their relations with the
committees. The research director feels that "girls
cannot work effectively with legislative committees.
They never arrive at authoritative positions."

37. Frederick H. Guild, "The Development of the
Legislative Council Idea," Annals of the American
Academy of Political and Social Sciences, CVC (1938),
144.

38. Guild interview.

39. See, for instance, Report and Recommendations of the Kansas Legislative Council, Part I, Tenth
Biennial Report submitted to the 1953 legislature,
Topeka, Kansas, December 15, 1952. This particular
report was supplemented by a second part. Charitable
and Benevolent Institutions and Mental Hospitals of the
State, Topeka, Kansas, December 15, 1952. The second
report was the product of "an exhaustive and intensive
study" emanating from a special legislative directive.

40. Rule 15.

41. "Facts about the Kansas Legislative Council,"
op. cit., p. 16.

42. Ibid.

43. Ibid.

44. F. H. Guild, "The Development of the Legisla-
Council Idea," op. cit., p. 146.

45. Ibid., pp. 146-147.

46. Rules 17, 18.

47. Editorial, Topeka Daily Capital, November 20, 1938, affords one of numerous available examples.

48. For an interesting and relevant discussion of leadership which bears on this point see J. A. C. Brown, The Social Psychology of Industry (Harmondsworth, Middlesex: Penguin, 1954), Ch. 8, "Leaders and Leadership," esp. pp. 222-225.

49. Ibid., p. 230.

50. Quoted from the Tao-Te-King, the Taoist scripture of China, in ibid., p. 225.

51. Guild interview.

52. "Facts," op. cit., p. 22.

53. Guild interview.

54. Ibid.

55. Ibid.

56. Ibid.

57. "Facts," op. cit., p. 22.

58. Memorandum, files of Research Department, Kansas Legislative Council, April 3, 1950, untitled, p. 1.

59. Ibid., pp. 1-2.

60. Guild interview.

61. Ibid.

62. Ibid.

63. Letter, Guild to Shumate, op. cit., p. 3-4.

64. Ibid., p. 4.

65. Ibid.

66. Ibid.

67. Guild interview.

68. Letter, Guild-Shumate, op. cit., p. 5.

69. Memorandum, Kansas Legislative Council files, no title, dated April 30, 1950, p. 2.

70. Ibid.

71. Guild interview.

72. See, for example, the laudatory treatment in Graves, State Government, pp. 257-261.

CHAPTER VI

1933-1958: A QUARTER-CENTURY OF GROWTH

The Michigan Legislative Council

A host of new members were swept into the
Michigan Legislature in the fall of 1932. They
took office in a time of great crisis, and struggled to get organized and to frame a program.
In this emergency the Speaker of the House
proposed a plan for a legislative council, which
was passed and approved by the Governor.[1]

In 1932 after 60 years of Republican domination the
Democrats captured control of Michigan state government, electing a governor, lieutenant-governor, all but
one of the other elective adminstrative officers, and a
sizeable majority of the legislators. Perhaps the most
inexperienced government in the history of the state
was confronted with some of its gravest problems.
Michigan was on the verge of financial collapse. Fifty-
four of the fifty-six Democrats in the House and a majority of the Senate were without any previous legislative experience. The public was crying for significant
legislation. At this point Speaker Bradley, one of two
experienced Democratic members of the House, proposed the establishment of a legislative council.[2]

Bradley's plan was based upon his knowledge of
the legislative council provision of the Model State Constitution.

The Michigan council contained nine members including the President of the Senate, Speaker of the
House, and three senators and four representatives

appointed by the presiding officers "in such a manner
as to assure bipartisan representation."[3]   It was to

> function during the interim between legislative
> sessions, . . . to prepare a legislative program
> . . . , to accumulate and compile such informa-
> tion as the council may consider useful . . . and
> to furnish such information to members of the
> legislature.[4]

The council was to develop a legislative program to deal
with the Michigan crisis. Five thousand dollars was appropriated and six council committees were appointed
to begin studies of specific problems in anticipation of
special legislative sessions. These committees contained non-council members of the legislature as well
as non-legislators appointed at the governor's recommendation.[5]

First committee reports appeared in November,
1933, in time for the special session which began that
month. Others appeared in 1934. But a newly-elected
governor opposed the council, and in 1935 proposed re-
peal of the law.[6] The council submitted no reports to
the 1937 legislature; no senators were appointed to it
that year, and in 1939 the act was repealed.

The Michigan council hardly survived the storm in
which it was born. At its very outset the "legislative
council movement" was marked by its most scintillant
success and one of its drearier failures.

The Spread of the Councils

From such mixed beginnings has come an impressive record of growth. By the beginning of 1958, according to the Council of State Governments, legislative
councils or "council-type" agencies were in operation
in 36 states. The states without such organizations are

TABLE 4

SPREAD OF COUNCILS AND "COUNCIL-TYPE AGENCIES"

Year	State	Title of Agency
1933	Kansas	Legislative Council
	Michigan	Legislative Council*
1936	Kentucky	Legislative Council*
	Virginia	Advisory Legislative Council
1937	Connecticut	Legislative Council
	Illinois	Legislative Council
	Nebraska	Legislative Council
	Pennsylvania	Joint State Government Commission
1939	Maine	Legislative Research Commission
	Maryland	Legislative Council
	Oklahoma	State Legislative Council
1943	Missouri	Committee on Legislative Research
	Wyoming	Legislative Interim Committee
1945	Alabama	Legislative Council
	Indiana	Legislative Advisory Commission
	Nevada	Legislative Commission
	North Dakota	Legislative Research Committee
1947	Arkansas	Legislative Council
	Minnesota	Legislative Research Commission
	Utah	Legislative Council
	Washington	State Legislative Council
1948	Kentucky	Legislative Research Commission
	Wisconsin	Joint Legislative Council
1949	Florida	Legislative Council
	South Carolina	Legislative Council
	Texas	Legislative Council
1951	New Hampshire	Legislative Council
	New Mexico	Legislative Council

TABLE 4—Continued

Year	State	Title of Agency
	South Dakota	Legislative Research Council
1952	Louisiana	Legislative Council
	Arizona	Legislative Council
	Colorado	Legislative Council
	Tennessee	Legislative Council Committee
1953	Alaska	Legislative Council
	Ohio	Legislative Service Commission
1954	Massachusetts	Legislative Research Council
	New Jersey	Law Revision and Legislative Services Commission
1955	Iowa	Legislative Research Committee
1957	Montana	Legislative Council

*Indicates organization later abolished.

Source: Book of the States 1956-1957, p. 120; Book of the States 1958-59, p. 70.

a relatively small minority, and it appears that the idea of the legislative council has become an accepted feature of American state government—as had the legislative reference agency some forty years earlier.

Causes of the Spread of the Councils

Nothing succeeds like success. The interest stimulated by the Kansas Legislative Council gave new meaning to earlier thinking on this subject. The grievous problems of the states and their legislatures and mounting pressures for centralization also stimulated interest in the council device. Finally the Council of State

Governments helped spread an awareness of the councils and related agencies.

Movements often begin slowly, gaining impetus as time passes. Only twelve legislative councils were established in the 1930's, including the short-lived Michigan and Kentucky organizations and the inoperative Rhode Island council. About two-thirds of the agencies were created during or after World War II. But the impact of the Kansas council was beginning to be felt within a couple of years after its establishment; by 1937 six additional states had established organizations based to some extent upon the Kansas experiment.

Each of these organizations, like others created later, was conditioned by the particular character of its setting. The Kentucky council was a product of the leadership of Governor A. B. "Happy" Chandler. "The Virginia Council was initiated by the governor and remains completely under his control insofar as composition and tenure of personnel are concerned."[7] Created in 1935 by executive order, it was dignified with statutory status in the following year at the governor's request. The Connecticut council was an outgrowth of the work of a commission which had studied the organization of the state government.[8] The Illinois council, discussed at length below, was the intriguing product of the imagination and political adeptness of a state legislator named T. V. Smith, a man who has also attained considerable renown in the academic profession. The Nebraska council was an adjunct of the unicameral legislature established in 1935. The council idea had, for that matter, long been espoused by Professor John P. Senning, a leading advocate of the unicameral legislature. He believed that

> the potential capacity for legislative leadership of a council made up of members from the lawmaking body is worthy of consideration. 'The

> successful use of this device indicates clearly
> the possibility of revitalizing legislative bodies
> within themselves. It has proved a substitute
> for the injection of vitality from outside.'[9]

By the beginning of World War II a variety of council models existed to serve as guides to interested states. By this time, too, the council idea was getting support from other sources. It had gained an established position in the literature on American state government, and was receiving increasing support from the Council of State Governments.

The Council in the Literature of State Government

The legislative council-on-paper preceded the legislative council-in-existence by a good twelve years, as we have noted. Prior to 1933 little was written about the council concept, although the 1926 edition of Arthur N. Holcombe's textbook, State Government in the United States, did make brief mention of it.[10]   By 1940 one finds the council mentioned in the "Third Edition Thoroughly Revised" of Ogg and Ray's ubiquitous Essentials of American Government, and in nearly all the standard texts on American state government— a good indication that the council idea had gained general acceptance among students of American government, although at the time there existed only ten organizations called legislative councils.

By 1940 a sizeable bibliography of material on the legislative council had accumulated. In all this writing the only caveat seems to have been the mild observation that the council device should not be regarded as a cure for all the inadequacies justly ascribable to our state legislatures.[11]

In its vast probing of the state of the nation's

resources, the National Resources Committee in 1938
had recommended that

> legislative councils be created by all the States
> that have not already done so; that existing sep-
> arate agencies in the form of legislative refer-
> ence bureaus, legislative counsel, and revisors,
> of statutes be made subordinate units of such
> councils; and that, where such agencies are not
> in existence, the statute setting up the council
> authorize that body to create divisions for the
> performance of their functions. Action in this
> way would eliminate, or obviate, duplication
> of organization and activities; give to the
> legislature a single strong body with the tech-
> nical officers having to do with research, bill
> drafting and codification, brought together in
> a single mutually helpful staff; and a centrali-
> zation of equipment in the form of a reference
> library, legislative records, and data regard-
> ing conditions in other jurisdictions. Prime
> responsibility for all work would rest with
> the council as a collegiate body, while im-
> mediate direction, supervision, and control
> over the staff would be exercised by an execu-
> tive secretary to the council who, it need hardly
> be said, should be a permanent officer.[12]

This recommendation, made when there was only
one well established legislative council, was both pre-
sumptuous and prescient. It did anticipate a tendency
toward the development and integration of legislative
service organizations which is, twenty years later, oc-
curring among some American states.

Meanwhile the gospel was carried across the land
by magazines ranging from scholarly journals to the
Rotarian and Business Week.[13] Kansas had shown the
way, and the term "council" as applied in this material
generally referred to or implied the Kansas model.
And it was held that through organizations of this type
the states could greatly improve the quality of legislative

decision-making. This writing understandably helped
lay a groundwork for the continued spread of the councils and related organizations in the years ahead.

Meanwhile the National Municipal League continued
to support the council idea. In the 1930's time caught
up with the League's almost inadvertent vision. Its early
legislative council proposal took on new pertinence, and
was in turn adapted somewhat to the emerging pattern of
of reality. The 1941 edition of the Model State Constitution contained explanatory articles on the council device by both Harold W. Dodds and Frederick Guild.[14]
The council had been retained in three successive ver-
sions of the model constitution; by 1945, on the basis of
experience in Kansas and elsewhere, a provision of that
document proposing executive representation on the
council which had been included since 1921 was finally
dropped.[15]

The Council of State Governments and the Legislative Council

The Council of State Governments has given more
impetus to the spread of the legislative councils and
"council-type" agencies than any other organization; the
value of its assistance in both the establishment and the
effective operation of councils and other state legislative service organizations has been substantial. The
very existence of this organization constitutes a significant difference between the early legislative reference
movement and the more recent spread of legislative
service organizations including councils.

The "legislative council movement" seems to have
captured the Council of State Governments, rather than
the opposite. As late as 1940 the Council was strongly
supporting legislative reference agencies as major means

to the improvement of the quality of state legislative work.[16] By 1946 the Council's Committee on Legislative Processes and Procedures issued a report whose 12-point program for improving state legislatures included a fairly strong endorsement of the legislative council—at the same time that it continued to espouse the importance of the legislative reference agency.[17]

The Council's position vis-a-vis the reference agencies went back to the days of Henry W. Toll and the American Legislators Association. One aim of that organization had been the establishment of an effective interstate legislative reference service, an undertaking which was most successfully performed by the Council. It has been in this capacity of service as a clearing-house of information and a ready source of consultative assistance that the Council of State Governments has contributed to the development of the legislative councils.

From the mid-'30's, the magazine, State Government, reported in detail upon the work of the legislative councils.[18] The Council became a major source of information on legislative councils and the experience of various states with them. To cite but one example, a member of the Council staff helped revise draft legislation providing for the establishment of the Kentucky Legislative Research Commission, the post-war successor to the ill-fated Kentucky Legislative Council of 1936.

The Council's field and research staff assist legislative councils and similar organizations in many ways— with information on the work, problems, and accomplishments of other organizations, and as a source of advice, recognition and encouragement. Since 1948 the Council of State Governments has sponsored an annual Legislative Service Conference, a four or five day meeting of legislators who are members of councils and other legislative service agencies, and of the staffs of such organizations, to stimulate interest in improved legislative organization and procedure.[19]

The Council of State Governments has hedged its bets. With all the help and encouragement it has given to legislative councils, it has avoided a position of favoring the council as the most suitable solution to the policy planning needs of state legislatures. It has supported reference agencies as well as councils, and to the Council of State Governments must go much of the credit for the previously noted renaissance of the legislative reference agencies.

Only the most dogmatic proponent of the legislative council could criticise this position. The relationship of the Council of State Governments to the legislative councils seems wise; certainly it is understandable. The Council is supported by the American states, by legislative appropriations. It must stand ready to help where it can. In view of the continued vitality of a variety of legislative service organizations, the Council could hardly favor one particular type at the expense of others. And if the Council has been somewhat imprecise in drawing distinctions between "true councils" and organizations labelled councils which are really not legislative councils, this is also understandable. The Council of State Governments is concerned with results and realities more than with scholarly abstractions.

The Spread of the Councils — and the Significance of Variations in the Emerging Pattern

Table 5 at the end of this chapter presents a fairly detailed picture of the development and current state of the American legislative councils — and "council-type agencies." As it suggests, there are councils and then again there are councils. The term legislative council has come to cover a variety of organizations with significant differences among them. These differences cropped up in the earliest days of the "council movement," and they have continued to be important. The most significant of them has been used as a basis for the preparation of the table itself; the agencies have been grouped into two categories—those which do and those which do not make recommendations to their respective legislatures. In the concept exemplified by the Kansas council the whole process aims at the preparation, submission and support of recommendations; the goal is preparation of a legislative program. But only 21 organizations called councils (or treated by the Council of State Governments as "council-type agencies") prepare such programs. The reasons behind the difference are most significant to an understanding of the legislative council in the American states.

At this point it cannot be said that the "legislative council movement" has run its course. There remain a number of states with no such organizations. In these and in other states prospects exist for further development or modification of legislative councils, "council-type agencies," and other service staffs of our state legislatures.

The record of a quarter-century suggests that a considerable ebb and flow will continue in the positions occupied by individual councils, although in some cases thoroughly stable arrangements appear to have developed in which there are well-balanced relationships between individual organizations and their settings.

The period during which the legislative councils emerged and spread was a time of great change and great trouble for the states, marked as it was by depression, war, and the new problems of the post-war period. Yet in this time no profound, or even radical, modifications occurred in the essential form or structure

of the American state legislatures. To this the unicameralism of the Nebraska experiment has proved an exception—and nothing more. The legislatures, like the
water jars of the Arabian Nights, have demonstrated
their ability to contain vastly varying contents with dif-
fering degrees of adequacy. Today one seldom finds the
crass and flagrant evils of the 19th Century, and the technical ineptitude of the turn of the century seems to have
been abated by such technical aids as bill drafting and
codification services. Meanwhile the states have become
junior—and limited—partners in the integrated enter-
prises of the New Federalism; and most of our legislatures appear to play roles other than that of creative
policy leadership in our subtle and complex system of
government.

In this context, in the past quarter-century, legislative councils emerged in Kansas and some other states
as a means of reasserting the role of legislative supremacy in the shaping of policy. At the very same time,
there has been a resurgence of a distinctly different
type of organization, the reference-type agency, whose
antecedants go back to the turn of the century, and whose
role is somewhat different than that of the council. The
two have developed side-by-side, as complementary
aspects of the most recent pattern of efforts to strengthen
our state legislatures. In a manner of speaking, the
"legislative council movement" has helped give rise to
a new legislative reference agency movement; and both
developments have been effectively nurtured by the
Council of State Governments.

Notes

1. Dean E. McHenry, The Legislative Council Idea (Berkeley: The University of California, December 1, 1934, p. 3.

2. Harold M. Dorr, "A Legislative Council for Michigan," American Political Science Review, XXVIII (April, 1934), pp. 270-275.

3. "An Act to create a legislative council. .. ," Michigan Public Acts, no 206 (1933).

4. Ibid.

5. See Charles W. Shull, "Legislative Council in Michigan," National Municipal Review, XXII (November, 1933), p. 570.

6. Guild, "The Legislative Council Idea," op. cit., p. 149.

7. George W. Spicer, "Gubernatorial Leadership in Virginia," Public Administration Review, I (Autumn, 1941), 448.

8. Report, Commission Concerning the Reorganization of the State Departments (Hartford, Connecticut, 1937), pp. 77-85. See also, "Connecticut Adopts Legislative Council," National Municipal Review, XXVI (May, 1937), 235.

9. John P. Senning, The One-House Legislature (New York: McGraw-Hill, 1937), p. 97. The quotation cited by Senning is from Rowell, "Responsible Legislative Leadership, State Government (June, 1934).

10. Holcombe, op. cit., pp. 526-527. It will be recalled that the author had participated in drafting the first Model State Constitution.

11. Harvey Walker, "Legislative Councils—An Appraisal," National Municipal Review, XXVIII (December, 1939), 841-842. See also his "Modernizing the State Legislature," The Rotarian, LIV (January, 1939), 22-23.

12. National Resources Committee, Research—a National Resource (Washington: Government Printing Office, 1938), p. 161.

13. Harvey Walker, "Modernizing the State Legislature," Rotarian, op. cit.; "Kansas Shows the Way," Business Week, December 4, 1937, p. 37. See also the January, 1938, issue of The Annals of the American Academy of Political and Social Science, which was devoted entirely to the state legislatures, and which included an excellent discussion of the Kansas council by Dr. Frederick H. Guild, "The Development of the Legislative Council Idea," at pp. 144-150. Other comments of the time will be found in these sources: Hubert Gallagher, "Legislative Councils," National Municipal Review, XXIV (March, 1935), 147-151; A. E. Buck, Modernizing Our State Legislatures (Pamphlet Series No. 4; Philadelphia: The American Academy of Political and Social Science, 1936); in a series of articles in the magazine State Government, cited below; and even in a mimeographed report on the legislative council prepared in 1939 by the Minnesota League of Women Voters. Thus the word spread.

14. Model State Constitution (3rd ed., New York, National Municipal League, 1941), pp. 22-24 and 30-32.

15. Model State Constitution (4th ed., New York: National Municipal League, 1945). Section 317 reads: "There shall be a legislative council consisting of not less than seven nor more than fifteen members, chosen by and from the legislature."

16. See for example, Eleanor V. Laurent's excellent study, Legislative Reference Work in the United States (Chicago: The Council of State Governments, 1939). For an earlier but still apparently valid reflection of the general position of the Council, see Brooke Graves, Uniform State Action, op. cit., esp. pp. vii-viii, 12-15, 57-61, and 281-304.

17. The Council of State Governments, Our State Legislatures (Chicago, 1946). A somewhat revised 1948 edition takes about the same general position, asserting that "provision for legislative councils or interim committees with adequate clerical and research facilities can be provided most readily and effectively through a legislative reference bureau." (Second page of an unpaged "Summary of Recommendations.") Somewhat erroneously the report asserts that "no legislature

that has established an adequate legislative reference
bureau has thereafter attempted to do without the service which it provides." (p. 15).

18. For example: Frederick H. Guild, "Legislative Councils in the Spotlight," XII (February, 1939),
26-27; "Legislative Councils," IX (June, 1936), 132;
"The Legislative Councils in Action," XVI (February,
1943), 34, 45-47; Chester H. Rowell, "Responsible Legislative Leadership," VII (June, 1934), 109; O. Douglas
Weeks, "Recent Developments in the State Legislative
Process," XVII (July, 1943), 162-166; Martha J. Zeigler,
"Legislators Work Between Sessions," X (November,
1937), 236-237. In addition to materials in its magazine, the Council has since 1939 published useful information on the councils in its biennially issued Book
of the States.

19. For a brief description of this conference, see
Book of the States 1954-55, pp. 12-13. In the name of
the Conference, the Council publishes a periodic Legislative Research Checklist, a useful summary of current
research activities of legislative service agencies.

LEGISLATIVE COUNCILS

A. Councils Making Legislative Recommendations; Total Number: 21

State	Agency	Date Established	Reference Library	Bill Drafting	Statute Revision	Bill and Law Summaries	Research Reports	Spot Research	Continuous Study of Finances	Budget Review	Legislative Post Audit
Alabama	Legislative Council	1945									
Alaska	Legislative Council	1953		*			*	*			
Arkansas	Legislative Council	1947	*	*		*	*	*	*	*(a)	
Connecticut	Legislative Council	1937	*			*	*	*			
Florida	Legislative Council	1949					*				
Kansas	Legislative Council	1933	*				*	*			
Maryland	Legislative Council	1939					*	*			
Montana (b)	Legislative Council	1957									
Nebraska	Legislative Council	1937	*	*		*	*	*	*	*	

TABLE 5—Continued

State	Agency	Date Established	Reference Library	Bill Drafting	Statute Revision	Bill and Law Summaries	Research Reports	Spot Research	Continuous Study of Finances	Budget Review	Legislative Post Audit
Nevada	Legislative Commission	1945									
	Legislative Counsel Bureau	1945					*	*			
New Hampshire	Legislative Council	1951					*				
North Dakota	Legislative Research Committee	1945	*	*	*		*	*			
Ohio	Legislative Service Commission	1953	*	*	*	*	*	*	*	*	
Oklahoma	State Legislative Council	1939		*		*	*	*			
Pennsylvania	Joint State Government Commission	1937	*		*		*	*			
South Dakota	Legislative Research Council	1951	*				*	*			

TABLE 5—Continued

State	Agency	Date Established	Reference Library	Bill Drafting	Statue Revision	Bill and Law Summaries	Research Reports	Spot Research	Continuous Study of Finances	Budget Review	Legislative Post Audit
Utah	Legislative Council	1947		*							
Virginia	Advisory Legislative Council	1936					*	*	*	*	
Washington	State Legislative Council	1947		*		*	*	*			
Wisconsin	Joint Legislative Council	1947					*				
Wyoming	Legislative Interim Committee	1949					*				

TABLE 5—Continued

B. "Councils and Council-Type Agencies" Not Making Legislative Recommendations; Total Number: 15

State	Agency	Date Established	Reference Library	Bill Drafting	Statute Revision	Bill and Law Summaries	Research Reports	Spot Research	Continuous Study of Finances	Budget Review	Legislative Post Audit
Arizona	Legislative Council	1953	*	*	*	*	*	*			
Colorado	Legislative Council	1953					*	*			
Illinois	Legislative Council	1937					*	*			
Iowa	Legislative Research Committee	1955					*				
Kentucky	Legislative Research Commission	1948	*	*	*	*	*	*	*		
Louisiana	Legislative Council	1952		*		*	*	*			
Maine	Legislative Research Committee	1939		*	*	*	*	*			
Massachusetts	Legislative Research Council	1954					*				

TABLE 5—Continued

State	Agency	Date Established	Reference Library	Bill Drafting	Statute Revision	Bill and Law Summaries	Research Reports	Spot Research	Continuous Study of Finances	Budget Review	Legislative Post Audit
Massachusetts (Cont.)	Legislative Research Bureau	1954					*	*			
Minnesota	Legislative Research Committee	1947	*				*	*	*	*	
Missouri	Committee on Legislative Research	1943	*	*	*		*	*			
New Jersey	Law Revision and Legislative Services Commission	1954		*	*	*	*	*			
New Mexico	Legislative Council	1951									
	Legislative Council Service	1951	*	*	*	*	*	*			
South Carolina	Legislative Council	1949	*	*		*	*	*			
Tennessee	Legislative Council	1953	*	*			*	*			

TABLE 5—Continued

State	Agency	Date Established	Reference Library	Bill Drafting	Statute Revision	Bill and Law Summaries	Research Reports	Spot Research	Continuous Study of Finances	Budget Review	Legislative Post Audit
Texas	Legislative Council	1949					*	*			

(a) Also responsible for preparing a state budget.
(b) Information not available.

* Source: Adapted from "Table 1, Permanent Legislative Service Agencies," and "Legislative Councils and Council-Type Agencies," Book of the States 1958–59, pp.61-69 and 70-71, respectively.

CHAPTER VII

FROM PRINCIPLES TO PRACTICE—
THE CLASSIC CASE OF THE ILLINOIS COUNCIL

The principles were laid down in Kansas. They found one of their earliest applications in Illinois. What happened is both interesting and revealing.

Establishment of the Illinois Council

Now as a newly elected member of the Illinois Senate—1934, it was—I was the victim of my own ignorance over and over compounded. It seemed to me that I knew nothing of all the innumerable things that as a legislator I needed to know. I was, in the first place, not a lawyer. I quickly discovered, partly as a result of this, that there was no use in trying to read the thousand-odd bills introduced into the State Senate, for I did not understand what I read. Nor had I one-tenth enough time to master them even if I had been much more adequate in comprehension. The business of a modern state is wide, and there seemed to be bills about everything of which I was ignorant. Dimly I discerned that other new members were in the same boat, though not often as paralyzed at the rudder as was I.

Begotten of my personal need, therefore, my desperate, my pathetic need, was the initial thought of introducing this bill. . . .[1]

Thus begins the story of the Illinois Legislative Council. Much time elapsed, however, before Senator Smith's bill—his only bill, it appears—became law. It

took two years for him to first establish himself with
members of the Illinois legislature as a "right guy."
The process involved a great deal of discretion, plus a
rare diversity of efforts.

> The first caucus of my party which I attended,
> without knowing a single soul, was already at
> the glasses, though not in its cups, when I ar-
> rived. The members seemed embarrassed
> at their reluctance to offer me a drink but not
> emboldened to overcome it. After a decent in-
> terval. I asked simply and naturally, if I might
> have a drink; and as somebody rushed to get
> me water for dilution, I poured a generous
> portion of (somebody else's) bourbon, and in-
> dulged myself neatly as an exiled Texan might.
> I thought nothing more of this. . . . I was told
> the next morning, however, by a friendly in-
> former, that the story was all over Capital
> Hill before midnight, and that I had made my-
> self more friends by that simple act than
> many elected idealists made in months. Hu-
> man relations in the legislature, as elsewhere,
> are indeed often composed of such flimsy, tri-
> vial, and sometimes unpraiseworthy stuff.

For a two-year period, Senator Smith's campaign
for the establishment of legislative council was essentially a campaign for the establishment of Senator Smith.

> Privately accepted as a friendly sort after the
> first night and publicly not disesteemed, . . .
> I held my oratorical breath for two years,
> traded votes, as the saying invidiously goes;
> talked privately especially with fellow-new-
> members about our joint predicament and
> how to cure or at least make tolerable our
> ignorance, and made friends among members
> old and new whenever I could be consistent
> with self-respect. Very little, believe me,
> goes on in trading votes or otherwise that

trenches upon the self-respect of any robust member.

Though a Democrat, I wrote speeches, especially radio speeches at which I was experienced, for a Republican Senator who was running for Governor. Though a member of the faculty of the University of Chicago, and being therefore investigated by the Senate Wallgreen Committee, I answered, behind the scenes, much of the mail received from the public by the Chairman of the Investigating Committee. He said that he did not know what to say, and trusted me to say the right thing.

The Chairman of that Committee called me from bed at the Capitol one post-midnight saying that he was in a 'hell of a fix'; that he had to take the train within an hour to Chicago to appear early next morning before the newsreel with President Hutchins and, I think, Mrs. Dilling. He declared pathetically that he did not know what to say. I asked what length his speech was to be, and then turned wide-awake by now to my faithful typewriter still sleepily lying by my side. . . . You would hardly expect that Senator or the Republican Senator running for the Governorship (would you?) to vote against my bill, any bill that I subsequently introduced.

And what would you expect a certain Italian Senator to do after several friendly passes, such for instance, as the one which I well recall? I went to him one day in a legislative lull, commented favorably on his tie and tailored suit. He looked glum and suspicious. I told him that I had a few months before been in Italy, his ancestral home. He said so what? I laid on heavily how the Italians were lovers of beauty, and how in that at least he was as good an Italian as I hoped he was American. 'What the hell are you driving at?' he demanded to know. 'Just this, Senator,' I amusedly replied. 'I have

the most beautiful girl in the stenographic pool
assigned to me, and she isn't worth a damn as
a stenographer. You have assigned to you, I
learn, the ugliest girl back there, but an excellent stenographer. I have much mail to
answer,' I went on, 'and you I suspect have
little.' 'None' he corrected. 'Then,' count-
ered I, 'What say—trade me your womanly
brains for my feminine beauty!' His hand
was out, his face wreathed in smiles, and his
words were happily in tune: 'You're on, Senator; you're on.' And so I was, not only on the
trade; but for this and other reasons which I
forget, I was on his list of friends. Embarrass-
ingly so in fact. He subsequently offered to
bump off anybody whom I would name for that
honor.

But getting through him to the bill itself: when
it had been introduced, two years later, and
was being railroaded to a dead-end committee
by an unsympathetic presiding officer, my Italian colleague rushed up to me whispering in
my ear that I stall the speaker for a few min-
utes until he could corral the Republican votes.
Quickly he returned and directed me to appeal
from the decision of the chair. Nobody was
more surprised than the speaker, nor anybody
more gratified than I, when the votes of the
opposition party snatched my bill from the
graveyard and sent it to a committee which
later gave it its place on the calendar of the
Senate—and a chance to be born.[2]

And born indeed was Senator Smith's bill, after a
continued series of alliances and strategic retreats, the
latter including a much reduced appropriation for the
Illinois Legislative Council—plus the perhaps more
painful sacrifice of a philosophic bill preamble admittedly couched in Benthamite terms.

Following its passage, the prospects for a healthy
future for Senator Smith's baby were by no means

auspicious. The Lieutenant Governor, who appointed the
Senate members of the council, appeared determined to
assure the failure of the organization. His appointments
included "John, the saloon keeper . . . good old inarti-
culate John," and "Joe, the vendor of I-know-not-what
behind the front of the flower shop"; according to Professor Smith "some of the House members were a little
better in promise."[3]

After passage, Smith suggested that the research
director of the Kansas council be brought in to help in
the organization of the Illinois council. Indeed, over his
initially outraged apposition, the first act of the Illinois
council's twenty-two members was a trip to Kansas to
observe the Kansas council—a junket which took much
of the $10,000 appropriation intended for the first bien-
nium's operation. This turned out not so unhappily. As
one of the council members pointed out, "he thought the
boys would like to have a trip out of the State, that they'd
learn something if they went to see whereas they would
not listen if we brought somebody up to speechify to
them. How right he was, I was soon to learn."[4]   And
out of this dizzy, haphazard, never-certain, and somehow typical legislative process evolved the Illinois Legislative Council, an organization which in twenty years of
continued activity has established a reputation for the
outstanding caliber of its work.

The act which resulted from this laborious and
sometimes agonizing process was patterned closely after the Kansas council.[5]   The Illinois council consists
of the presiding officers of the two houses, plus ten
senators appointed by the president of the senate and
ten representatives appointed by the Speaker of the
House, with party representation "to be in proportion
generally to the relative numbers of members of the
political parties in each House of the General Assembly."[6]   The duties of the council were described in a

manner quite comparable to those of the Kansas organization. Explicitly included was a mandate "to prepare
such legislative program in the form of bills or otherwise, as in its opinion the welfare of the State may require." [7]

The legislative council's research department was
organized in June, 1938.[8] From the beginning it was
staffed by men of exceptional ability. Soon after its organization, the council decided that its reports would be
submitted to the General Assembly "without recommendation." In these two circumstances one finds the essence of the Illinois Legislative Council.

Professor Charles M. Kneier of the University of
Illinois was the first Director of Research. He came to
the council in 1938, accompanied by Jack Isakoff, in-
structor in political science and part-time council secretary. Professor Kneier accepted the council research
directorship with the understanding that the position
would be temporary. After a few months he returned to
the University and was succeeded by a series of three
well trained men, the last of whom, Dr. Isakoff, the current Director, took office late in 1939.[9]

The Illinois Council's decision not to submit a legislative program was made after the first biennium of
council operations, during which the modus operandi of
the council gradually took form.

In 1937 the council had been given ten research assignments. One concerned the reapportionment of circuit courts in Illinois, a matter which was given thorough
and expensive attention by council members, who made
it a point to actually travel the circuits at state expense,
—an action which led to some criticism. After paying
all of the council's travel expenses only $ 3,000 re-
mained for research, and the salaries of professors
Kneier and Isakoff were paid in part from the funds of
the Illinois Legislative Reference Bureau.

The council encountered additional difficulties during this first biennium. One of its members responsible
for supervising the council's finances proved rather lax
in the expenditure of state funds. He bought typewriters
without bothering to secure an exemption from the state
tax. He also bought a set of golf clubs. At any rate,
legislative sentiment toward the council in the first session following its establishment was decidedly mixed.
On one hand, there was recognition that the council's research work was "pretty good and useful." On the other
hand, activities of the council members had engendered
resentment. Furthermore, some criticism was voiced
during the 1939 legislative session that the organization
was "attempting to do the thinking for the entire body"
and "assuming the position of a 'little legislature.'"[10]

For a time it appeared that the council would be
abolished by the neat procedure of failing to appropriate
any funds. An appropriation was, however, secured, and
the legislature itself took no overt steps to intervene in
the council's policy of operations.[11]

At its first meeting following the session, looking
back over the mingled experience of the biennium, the
council decided "more or less unanimously" that in the
future it would restrict itself to research and reference
activities and would not engage in the formulation of
legislative proposals.[12] According to Mr. Isakoff; "I
don't think the council was ever very eager to make recommendations."

So it was that over a period of perhaps five years
Mr. Smith's dream was conceived, delivered, and set
adrift in the whirling stream of legislative life. As not
uncommonly happens in such cases, a combination of
heredity and environment triumphed over the dream of
one parent, who might later have questioned the legitimacy of the child he had helped spawn. Insofar as Mr.
Smith had envisioned a legislative council which would

emulate Kansas and serve as a focal point of legislative planning and leadership through the continued preparation of a legislative program, his vision had been faulty. The Illinois council became something other than its father's child; but this is not to deny its merit.

The Operation of the Illinois Council

The Illinois Legislative Council, as originally envisioned, was to work after the model of the Kansas council, which recommends bills to the Kansas legislature.

The Illinois council, however, has not usually sponsored legislation. Instead it has received proposals from members of the legislature, referred them to the research department with an indication as to the scope of the research study expected, approved the resulting research report, and left it largely to the initiative of the sponsor of the proposal or of other interested legislators to introduce bills that might seem to be indicated by research studies. These research studies have not recommended legislation, although sometimes they have indicated possible alternatives for legislative action.[13]

The Illinois Legislative Council and the Kansas Legislative Council can more readily be contrasted than compared. One makes recommendations while the other does not. As a result, the relationships of the research departments to the councils and of the councils to the legislatures differ radically.

The stated aim of the Illinois agency is to provide reference plus analysis for the individual legislator in response to his own felt need. "The Council's objective is to help the legislators, mostly as individuals, to do their own jobs."[14] Thus to judge the Illinois council in

terms of its effectiveness as a legislative programming
agency, a la Kansas, is to criticise an apple for failing
to taste like an orange.

The Function of the Council Proper

The council process begins with the introduction of
proposals for study. Council participation in planning
or initiating project proposals is, however, limited.
Members receive no remuneration for council work except
a ten-cent a mile travel allowance for attending meetings. "For years the Illinois council has met for one
day only, four times a year, as required by the statutes.
We spend about half the time having lunch."[15]

In Illinois a tradition has developed under which a
council member, once appointed, continues to be reappointed so long as circumstances permit. As a result of
the legal requirement that members be divided proportionately between the two parties, it occasionally becomes necessary to replace a council member in order
to maintain the required political balance on the council.

"The council conscientiously regards as one of its
major functions insulating the research staff from policy
influence and protecting it against what might be regarded as invidious politics."[16] The Illinois Legislative
Council is an organ of protection and control. It nomi-
nally, directs and regulates the activities of the council
staff. Undoubtedly the council with its experienced legislative members has protected the research organization; the likelihood of attack on the staff and its work is
reduced by the very existence of the council.

The reports of the research department are subject
to review by the council prior to publication. One
gathers, however, that the council exercises no strong
positive control over the research staff or its products.

The Illinois Legislative Council does maintain a
series of standing committees.[17] They exist "almost on

paper," except for that on council finance and budget
which does review administrative reports periodically
submitted by the research director.

The contrast between Illinois and Kansas is clear.
The Illinois council does not serve as a means of integrating pre-session study and legislative decision-
making; it does not attempt systematically to synthesize
technical facts and political judgments, to digest and
convert to a program the materials with which the legislature must deal. Research rather than synthesis is the
key element of the Illinois Legislative Council.

The Research Department and Its Operation

From its beginnings, the competence of the Illinois
council research staff has been extraordinarily high—
probably as good as will be found in any council in the
United States.[18]

The organization is rather small, consisting of a
director, assistant director, about four research analysts,
and as many clerks. The research analysts are individuals with graduate training in government and/or law.
(After joining the council staff, its director supplemented
his Ph.D. in political science with a law degree.)

Salaries in the organization are quite good in com-
parison with the prevailing level of pay to be found in
Illinois, and certainly on a par with those paid in other
legislative councils. Research analysts receive from
$350 to $500 per month or more. The salary of the director is in excess of $10,000 per year. The political
neutrality of the council's research and clerical staff
has been consistently maintained.[19]

The research department makes occasional use of
consultants. The three former directors of research,
Dr. Kneier, Chairman of the Department of Political
Science, University of Illinois, Dr. R. G. Browne, now

with the Teacher's College Board of the State of Illinois, and Dr. Orville Alexander, Head of the Department of Government at Southern Illinois University, serve as unpaid consultants. They are "nice to have. . . . We glory in their names." Their contribution to the organization consists of occasional help in the recruitment of staff members and in informal suggestions about tentative or planned research projects. From time to time the council also engages technical consultants in connection with specific studies.

The council's research organization has over the years compiled an impressive record of productivity. In one recent year 18 formal research reports were issued, plus three newsletters describing council activities and developments of possible interest to the members of the legislature, as well as 333 typewritten "informational responses."[20] This represents a typical year's output.

> All proposals for research reports shall be presented to the Council in writing by a member of the legislature. Such proposals shall have a descriptive title and bear the name of the sponsor. Any member of the legislature shall be privileged to attach to this proposal any supplementary matter which he believes will be of help to the Council.[21]

The process of initiating research studies in Illinois, unlike Kansas, is quite simple. No legislative approval is required. Proposals may be submitted at any time.[22] The council ostensibly passes upon all proposals before any action begins in the research department, and is free to bury them without recourse, although in practice this seldom happens.[23] The council leans heavily upon recommendations and suggestions from the director. "The main job of the council is to say: Full report, bulletin, or memo—and to dictate priorities.'"[24]

In its relation to research assignments, the council

performs a dual function: It protects the research department against requests which might overload it or
perhaps involve it in activity which might be politically
unwise at the time. It also places an <u>imprimatur</u> upon
the work of the research department, thereby conferring
upon it the status of more-or-less unquestioned acceptability by the legislators.

Once an assignment has been made the council research staff is free to pursue the matter with no further
recourse to the council until completed. It is then
cleared with the latter body which retains control over
release of the research department's reports.[25] This
review and approval for release in no way constitutes
the adoption of any policy position regarding a matter
about to come before the legislature. For that matter,
council approval constitutes no assurance that the subject of a report will be brought before the General Assembly in the form of a bill. In practice, clearance is
usually a matter of form although there are occasional
exceptions. Practical responsibility lies with the director of research to bring to the attention of council members material about which they might have qualms or
questions.

In each case the responsibility of the research department is for the preparation of a "fact-finding study
and report."[26] This mandate is at times interpreted as
permitting the statement of alternative approaches to a
given problem, along with a tentative analysis of each
possible course of action.

The ceaseless quest for objectivity in the research
program of the Illinois council poses its problem. In
Illinois as in Kansas one senses a persistent awareness
of the need for freedom from ostensible bias. One purpose of the council proper is to serve as a many-headed
guardian of the objectivity of the research department's
reports. And while this is more a latent than overt

function, its significance must not be overlooked. By its
very presence the council helps protect against the likelihood—and thus the consequences—of rash departures
from the realm of fact-finding.

The products of the council's research department
are not those of an intellectual eunuch. Many reports—
particularly the research memoranda—are purely factual, i.e., thoughtful, carefully organized collections of
pertinent data; others go further.[27] The council's research studies are an impressive demonstration of dedication to the criterion of objectivity—as well as a
good illustration of the meaning of this sacred term in
the field of legislative research. Council reports frequently incorporate, in lieu of suggestions or recommendations, summaries of the existing statutes or arrangements found in other state governments which bear upon
the problem under consideration.[28]

Much of the research work of the Illinois council is
analytical as well as descriptive. Any analytical approach goes beyond "fact-finding" in the narrowest
sense of that term. Analysis involves determinations of
what is significant, and culminates in conclusions. In
Illinois the latter are always limited or tentative. They
are often stated as alternatives, carefully couched to
avoid the appearance of recommendations. To take an
example:

> A number of alternative courses of action are
> available for consideration if the General As-
> sembly should determine that existing Illinois
> provisions for verification of election returns
> have shortcomings and that the practice of
> other states suggest some desirable amend-
> ments. Attention could be given to providing
> more extensive verification procedures in the
> course of the canvass and largely on the initia-
> tive of the election authorities, or there could
> be a chance to improve contest provisions of

the election laws by including specifications as to
recounts in connection with such contests, or there
could be adopted a recount system which is not independent on a formal contest. Indeed, some combination of each of these approaches might be feasible.[29]

Cautious phrasing is the hallmark of this work. It
is supported by a calm and lucid description of procedures for verifying election results in Illinois and elsewhere. The study does not focus upon a definition of a
problem avowed to exist in Illinois; rather it asserts the
importance of procedures for verifying election results,
describes the methods involved, discusses the merit and
disadvantages of a simplified election recount procedure,
outlines what would be involved in action by Illinois to
modify its recount law, and poses the above-cited alternatives. The dispassionate and erudite report is thought-
fully prefaced by a simple three-page summary.

The study, like many others made by the council
staff, poses these implicit questions to its recipients:
How significant is this subject? Is there need for action
on the matter? Given an affirmative answer to the latter question, the report furnishes some guides.

Such an approach will occasionally be transcended,
but only in non-controversial, procedual matters.

Thus has the research department successfully maintained its protective cloak of objectivity. More important than the question of whether its products have been
truly "objective" is the fact that they have been consistently accepted as such. In the tumultuous legislative
world abstract speculation upon the nature of objectivity
and its attainability is less significant than failure to be
objective—or, more specifically, than to err, misrep-
resent or be deomonstrably partial. The absence of
taint in Illinois is a tribute to the research department
and its inimitable director; since the council's active
participation in research is limited indeed, the

brunt of responsibility for its quality—and hence for the
survival of the organization—lies here.

The Council and the Legislature

The legislative council and the general assembly
are linked through the distribution of council reports and
by the informal personal relations of the Director of Research with members of the legislature. Major research
reports are distributed to all members of the assembly.
The more numerous memorandum reports are customarily distributed only to council members, the legislator
asking for the study, and to others immediately concerned, although additional distribution sometimes occurs.[30]

The research department periodically sends a newsletter to all members of the general assembly, informing them of current studies as well as other matters of
presumed interest. This often leads to requests from
individual legislators for council memoranda. At the
end of each fiscal year, the council submits an annual
report to the legislature, the bulk of which summarizes
current research studies. The Illinois council makes no
effort to limit access to its reports. Legislators are
encouraged to make the fullest possible use of them, as
well as the total facilities of the organization; the prime
aim in limiting the distribution of many materials prepared in the research department is to avoid swamping
individual members of the assembly with unsought papers on subjects of little or no interest.

To the extent that a supply is available, copies of
research reports and memoranda are distributed to interested individuals outside the legislature. A council rule
requires that copies of each major report be distributed
"to all elected state officers and to the heads of the
major departments of the state government."[31] And

while, according to its director, the council staff is
made up of "people with a passion for anonymity," this
does not mean that council reports are not distributed
to the press. In public relations the council rather than
the research department is understandably featured.

To characterize and assess the relation of the research director to the legislators is not easy, for this is
a highly personal matter. He appears to be liked and
trusted, and his sometimes delicate and confidential as-
sociations with individual legislators have posed no major difficulties for his organization.

One of the director's not infrequent session-time
problems is fending off requests for opinions concerning
the merit or demerit of specific legislative proposals.
His position does not permit him to take sides; yet he
has an obligation to be helpful. The research department therefore stands ready to furnish arguments for or
against a given proposal on a confidential basis to any
individual legislator requesting either or both. In so doing the department disavows any identification with a
policy position but merely "provides objective assistance." The rules of this subtle game have come to be
accepted in Illinois—a tribute to the quality of the
Illinois council's director of research.

> Sec. 8. The recommendations of the council
> shall be completed and made public at least
> thirty days prior to any sessions of the Gen-
> eral Assembly at which such recommenda-
> tions are to be submitted and a copy of said
> recommendations shall be mailed to the post
> office address of each member of the Gen-
> eral Assembly, to each elective State of-
> ficer, and to the State Library.[32]

The dead letter of this law is a fitting introduction
to the question of the impact of the Illinois Legislative
Council upon the general assembly. This is certainly

more difficult to discern and assess than in Kansas, and
with its refined, systematic council process explicitly
geared to the operations of the legislature. The effective
purpose of the Illinois council is at variance from both
the intent of its original proponent and the statute under
which it exists. According to the somewhat broadly
stated rationale of the Illinois council, "The individual
legislator still counts, and he needs help. The council's
objective is to help the legislators, mostly as individuals,
to do their own jobs."[33]

Nothing highlights more sharply the difference between Kansas and Illinois than the focus of the one organization upon legislature as an institution or functioning body, and the avowed orientation of the other toward
the individual legislator. The Illinois council is not an
essential adaptation or extension of the legislative process; it is a professed effort to make that process more
effective by making the individual legislator more effective, and in this sense is an application of the older
reference bureau concept of "more rational policy making through research." Both Illinois and Kansas proceed
from the postulate of the amateur "citizen legislator";
once past this point there is an abrupt parting of the
ways.

The Illinois council has attempted to assess its impact upon the legislature.[34] An analysis of 325 proposals
for council studies submitted by individual legislators
between March, 1938, and May, 1950, indicated that
eighty per cent of the completed proposals for council
study had been followed by the introduction of one or
more bills on the subject under study by either the sponsor of the proposal or another legislator. In the case of
major research publications, the record indicates that
only 7.4 per cent of such reports were "unlinked to bills
introduced." There appears to be little question about
the pertinence of the council's research.

The impact of the council—or more explicitly of
its research department—upon the legislators is also
attested by steady demands for assistance. Between
1938 and 1950 more than 1,000 requests for information
or related assistance were received from individual
legislators. "A minimum of four out of every five members of the 67th General Assembly have been aided directly and specifically at some time during their service in the legislature. . . ."[35]

The workload of the Illinois council has grown slowly
and steadily throughout the period of its existence; the
director currently receives requests for a wide variety
of services from individual legislators, "ranging from
speech material to arguments in favor of or against a
given measure, from help in handling a technically complicated inquiry from a constituent to somehow arranging for the reproduction of 150 copies of a letter." [36]
The council staff has come to be regarded by legislators
as a major source of miscellaneous assistance as well
as an almost unique clearing house of accurate information on practically any phase or problem of government
in Illinois. "At times we seem to get to be a kind of office of miscellaneous service and information."

The existence of the council has not eliminated the
use of interim commissions or committees in Illinois.
In fact, the use of such devices appears to have grown
since the council was created. In 1937 the Illinois legislature established a joint budgetary commission which
"performs a kind of legislative budget-making function,
and does employ an accountant."[37] Since 1937 the legislature has also established two permanent interim commissions, the Motor Vehicle Laws Commission and the
Commission to Visit State Institutions. The former presented a legislative program in 1953, and the latter
group submitted a report with recommendations. In
neither case were bills introduced as commission

legislation. Other interim commissions in Illinois pre-
sently maintain quasi-permanent status. Some of them
"have become established as clearing houses for certain
kinds of legislation." Each session of the General Assembly results in the establishment of additional temporary interim committees, which cease to exist with
the beginning of the following legislature.

"The interim commissions are invariably staffed,
and sometimes do initiate legislation," although "responsibility for introducing legislative proposals is invariably individual rather than collective."[38] The council research staff maintains informal working relationships
with interim commissions to the extent that the latter
seek assistance. No systematic pattern has developed,
however, nor does one seem likely to do so. The position
of neutrality and impartiality maintained by the council,
plus the fact that interim commissions usually prefer to
procure their own staffs, suffice to maintain a cleavage.
In discussing the relationships between the council and
interim commissions, the council research director
pointed out that

> if the interim commission can focus on a prob-
> lem, it can probably get more money to study it
> than the council might be able to; and then,
> there is the matter of representation— in
> other words, the appointment of expert or
> specifically interested people from the legis-
> lature to serve on commissions which are
> studying particular problems.

A few years ago the council's research director
was placed in charge of research for the Illinois " Little Hoover Commission," as the Shaefer Commission
on the Organization of Illinois government was called.
In this capacity he was required to delineate issues and
questions as a basis for policy recommendations. Even
here, however, a relatively successful effort was made

to draw the line between research and recommendation through the use of task force reports which stopped at the point of listing alternatives.

Since 1913 the Illinois General Assembly has been served by a Legislative Reference Bureau. According to the council's rules, "it shall be the duty of the Research Department to cooperate with the Legislative Reference Bureau in any request made by the Bureau."[39] In practice, relations between the council and the bureau are "good—if limited." The bureau concentrates almost entirely upon bill-drafting. "Its people are regarded as legal experts of the top caliber. It does not impinge upon the council nor does the council impinge upon it."[40]

One final point concerning the details of the relationship between the council and the legislature: There has been little contact between the council and the staff of the Senate, although the council's research department performs some service activities for the House, including scheduling of committee hearings and the reproduction of committee reports. The council also assists the legislature by publishing a legislative manual, largely a book of rules, plus a directory of Illinois state officers.

Council-Executive Branch Relations

"The council is a legislative agency, rather than part of the executive branch of the government."[41] Technically this is incorrect, although for all practical purposes the statement is valid. The council appears to be subject to regular state statutes governing civil service according to a ruling by the attorney general some years ago; and it is subject to the same budgetary process as other governmental agencies in Illinois. Conceivably the governor could eliminate the council or at least its research department through his item veto power over appropriations.

The council is not a significant factor in the relationships between a relatively powerful chief executive and the legislature. On the other hand, the legislative position of the governor is an important consideration in an appraisal of the council.

> The Governor of Illinois, whether or not his party controls the Legislature, has more opportunity to influence legislative action than any other outside source. The veto power, surely the most important of his controls, includes an item veto over appropriation measures and goes virtually unchallenged. The Governor is the only non-member of the legislature with a continuous and direct access to the General Assembly starting with a biennial message that the Constitution directs him to submit to the legislature at the convening of each session, and continuing through the session with legislative leaders of both houses. He is required to and does submit an executive budget. . . Finally, he is the head of the political party that expects the bulk of patronage, and he can be personal dispenser of patronage if he so chooses.[42]

The Illinois governor is a potent legislative force. The extent of gubernatorial influence varies, but an unassailable tradition of positive executive leadership exists, and has long been accepted by the legislature. Its extent was indicated in 1953,

> . . . when the General Assembly passed bills providing for 30 legislative interim commissions to study particular problems and report to the 1955 session. Appropriations to these commissions would have totaled four times the amount allotted to such activities in the executive budget. Accordingly, the Governor vetoed half of the bills involved, in most instances noting the availability of existing

legislative service agencies to undertake the
project proposed. Plainly a nice question of
legislative-executive relationships and the
propriety of the exercise of the veto power
is raised by gubernatorial denial of authority
and funds to the legislature to establish a
committee of its own members to study a
legislative problem.[43]

The Illinois council is a particular product of its
setting and circumstances. Strong gubernatorial leadership is the key fact in that setting. The rapid shift of
the Illinois council from a recommendatory position to
a more innocuous approach really requires a stronger
explanation than the peccadilloes of the council during
the first months of its existence.

Law-making is a part-time occupation for all
but a few members of the Illinois General Assembly. Participation in legislative activity
is neither sufficiently demanding, sufficiently
lucrative, nor sufficiently secure for members to abandon professional or business interests. Consequently, one of the most striking phenomena in the Illinois legislative houses
is the continuing struggle of the members, as
individuals, to find a satisfactory adjustment
between their public and private pursuits.[44]

Those ambivalent amateurs, the citizen legislators,
are not lacking in policy leadership—leadership from
many sources, some of them quite conflicting, and several
substantially external to the legislature itself. In particular,

legislative leadership is forthcoming from the
governor of Illinois. The Senate majority whip
described the procedure during the 1953 session: 'Every Monday night, the Speaker of the
House, the majority leader of the House, the
majority whip of the House, the President pro

tem of the Senate meet with the Governor on
the subject of legislation pending or proposed,
in connection with which we generally invite
the proponents of any particular measure that
is then very current, or the chairman of the
committee before which some special and
legislation is pending. We go over the legislation, its potentialities, its possibilities,
whether it is feasible, whether it is desir-
able, and we thresh it out as well as we
know how.'[45]

In Illinois there is not room for a leadership process of the type represented by the Kansas council. In
its struggle to find a legitimate place for itself, the
Illinois council quickly gravitated toward dispassionate
research. A void existed to be filled despite the presence of the legislative reference bureau. The council
has been criticized for its unwillingness to draft legislative programs and its failure to eliminate the use of
special interim commissions. But such criticism does
not appear to be realistic.

You can't have bi-partisan relationships and
retain the confidence of the various governors
if your agency embarks on the formulating of
policies. By holding rigidly to fact-finding
and research, the Council has avoided this.
Furthermore, I think in Illinois we have
learned that special legislative commissions
are very important for reconciling various
interests and for developing a better information among the legislators on particular
problems. The Legislative Council can successfully perform this function on scores of
topics not referred to special commissions.
Of course, special commissions are able to
make recommendations because they have
concentrated upon a single problem.

I have worked in Illinois State Government
long enough to believe that we have developed

procedures that function very well. I think the
Legislative Council has contributed to this;
certainly the special commissions have. The
result is that both the legislature and the governor have a very friendly attitude toward
legislative fact-finding and research.[46]

The Illinois Council—A General Evaluation

The Illinois council is <u>not</u> a legislative council in
the sense that the Kansas council is. Instead, the Illinois council fulfills more than adequately the basic function and purpose of the legislative reference bureau as
visualized decades earlier by Dr. Charles McCarthy of
Wisconsin. It is probably a more effective legislative
research agency than most of the reference organizations created during the early period of legislative reference bureau growth.[47]

The Illinois council has been effective beyond question. The Illinois legislature still has its log-jams, and
what happens in them is apparently little different than
in the past.[48] No one asserts that the quality of the bulk
of Illinois legislation has shown marked improvement
since 1937. In general, the legislative process is what
it has traditionally been. But on some matters, including most of the complex and important subjects of legislation, the legislature, or at least some of its members,
are well informed. The existence of an impartial source
of accurate information has reduced the span of opportunity for flagrantly irresponsible assertions and action.
The legislators have a place to turn for aid—a resource which at least removes an impediment to their
individual effectiveness to the extent they choose to use
it. And, as individuals, many of them use it.

Kansas versus Illinois

The Illinois council has grown from an organization with an annual appropriation of $10,000 to one with a budget of over $100,000.[49] The quality of its research is a legitimate object of respect. But if we are to deal with fact-finding this final fact remains: The Illinois council is no "little legislature." It does contribute a degree of focus to the legislative process, but this focus is the spotlight of research; it is not the systematic, deliberate synthesis of fact and judgment and the pre-meditated formulation of an explicit program of action. The Kansas council operates at the very heart of the legislative process; the Illinois council more near the periphery. Each organization has its raison d'etre and its place. What has, however, not often been made clear is the fact of the essential difference. To apply the term "legislative council" to both Kansas and Illinois is to include Gina Lollobrigida and an Irish washer-woman in the same category. Both have their merits and their similarities, but the failure to make an appropriate distinction leaves much to be desired.

The distinction itself raises the question: why the difference? The answer lies in the settings of the two organizations. The Illinois legislative council and the Kansas legislative council each represent something of an "ideal type."

The partisan make-up of the Illinois and Kansas legislatures are likewise matters of high contrast, Kansas being staunchly and persistently Republican and Illinois marked by a two-party tradition.[50] Is this the essential fact in an explanation of the difference between the Kansas and the Illinois councils? It would be satisfying to be able to assert conclusively that "one-party legislature = program council; two-party legislature = research agency."

There is some validity in such an explanation. Consider, for instance, the fact that a legislative council is appointed at the close of a legislative session and assigned the development of a legislative program for submission after the next general election. An intervening upset in partisan (or factional) control of the legislature would produce a situation in which a program prepared under the leadership of one group would be submitted to a legislature under the control of another. To perceive the difficulties which might inhere in such circumstances it is not necessary to assume substantial differences of principle or program between the groups. Often in politics issues involve matters of sponsorship and credit as much—if not more than—the content of proposals.

A persistent pattern of one party legislative organization and control does suggest a substantial degree of homogeneity in the legislature and its general outlook.[51] But, by itself,

> one-partyism, as measured by formal attach-
> ment to a single party, is by no means a satis-
> factory indicator of political homogeneity for
> within southern one-party states from time to
> time deep and abiding cleavages make them-
> selves manifest in the primary vote.[52]

Kansas has for decades been a strongly Republican state. Although its governorship has been captured three times by the Democrats since 1930, the Kansas legislature has not been under the control of the Democratic party for many years. Kansas politics, substantially free of any rural-urban bipolarization, tend to fit Key's description of

> the strand of rural and small-town politics
> [which] contributes a special color and tone
> to the American political system. . . . Such

> a politics is predominantly a one-party poli-
> tics which is reflective of a highly integrated
> community life with a powerful capacity to
> induce conformity. In those areas party as
> such often has no meaning as a combination
> to fight the opposition. It is rather an ex-
> pression, continued from generation to
> generation, of the consensus of a majority
> in such overwhelming command that it is
> unaware of any challenge to its position. . . .
> The politics of the locality is a politics of
> personality and of administration rather than
> a politics of issues. The issues have long
> been settled and the outcome embodied in a
> durable equilibrium of power and status with-
> in the community.[53]

If this be Kansas, it follows that within the legislature there exists a relatively calm and stable basis for
approaching the issues. Policy questions admittedly
exist, but one finds much less of a tendency toward persistent, structured political cleavages. Such a context
facilitates the operation of a legislative council in a
number of ways, all of them reflections of political continuity and cohesion. This allows room for a considerable degree of rational examination of policy issues,
and for the give-and-take of compromise within a framework of agreement on fundamentals. Such a circum-
stance is not a simple function of a single party politics
but of a single party politics resting upon "the consensus of a more or less undivided community or at least
of a majority in . . . overwhelming command."

In Illinois one finds neither the single party politics
nor the underlying sense of homogeneity. This is not a
simple matter of "Democratic and metropolitan Chicago arrayed against a rural, Republican downstate. . . .
Illinois outside of Chicago is not all of the same piece
politically."[54] At the same time, "The cleavage between metropolitan residents and rural and small-town

dwellers has become a most significant foundation for
dual systems of state politics."[55]

Illinois represents a good example of what Key describes as the "Frustration of Party."

> Our orthodox doctrines of constitutionalism
> justify a bit of friction between governors and
> legislators. . . . [But] a mixture of stubborn
> independence and statesmanlike collaboration
> between the branches of government works
> well only so long as the proportions of the in-
> gredients are correct.[56]

The essential idea of the legislative council as a
participant in policy-making rests upon the acceptance
of the separation of powers concept; it also assumes a
considerable degree of harmony in relations between
governor and legislature, and considerable power over
policy vested in the latter. In Illinois during six of the
22 years between 1931 and 1953 one party controlled
the governorship while the other commanded one or
both houses of the legislature. In the absence of a
thorough analysis of the politics of Illinois state government and their application to the legislature, Key's description of the following phenomena seems applicable:

> . . . the formal organs of government. . .
> [operate]. . . in a field of influences which
> may react on them and condition, even alter,
> their roles in the formally ordained consti-
> tutional system. The governor who must
> more or less regularly face an opposition
> legislature tends to be thrown with special
> force into a role of representation of those
> sectors of the electorate upon which he de-
> pends most obviously for popular majorities.
> Often . . . he must depend on urban majori-
> ties while the legislature looks countryward.

> Further, the relations between the formal

governmental structure and its matrix of influences may both mold behavior and fix the
status of the legislative body. Many factors
have conspired to produce the low status of
American state legislatures. Yet, among
these factors, its unrepresentative character must be assigned a high rank. A body
that often acts reluctantly under executive
pressure and whose chief purpose often seems
to be one only of negation cannot but in the
long run lose prestige. A body that is con-
demned by its constitution to the defense of a
partial interest in the state becomes, if not a
council of censors, something other than a representative body in the conventional sense.[57]

The Illinois legislature possesses little of the homogeneity one finds in Kansas. The politics of Illinois
involves cleavage and struggle. The governor is forced
into a major role as representative. There is no neat
functional delineation between chief executive and representative assembly. In such circumstances one
does not find much basis for a program-oriented legislative council, and rapid response of the Illinois Legislative Council to the inexorable force of political reality
is less than a surprise. Not having a "legislature"
with which to work—in the sense of the Kansas legislature—the council turned to its members.

Finally, one essential iteration is in order: A critical element in the survival and success of the Illinois
council has been its director of research. The Illinois
and Kansas councils are in many ways antipodal, but in
this respect they are the same: neither is simply an
impersonal combination of structure and function; the
existences of both have been inseparably linked with individual men, each of whom has played a critical role.
In Illinois as in Kansas much more than impersonal
process is involved in the functioning of the legislative
council; process per se cannot include the unique

integrity, competence, and personality of a particular
person, nor can it assure the contiuation of an activity
or an organization in the absence of a strategic individual. Recognizing this, it is unwise to speak simply of
the mechanical transplantability of such organizations
as the Illinois council and the Kansas council— or even
to assume the unchanged continuance of these organizations beyond the terms of their current directors of research.

Notes

1. T. V. Smith, "The Biography of a Bill, " the text
of an address to the Legislative Service Conference,
New Orleans, Lousiana, September 28, 1953, p. 1. One
hardly need identify the eminent political philosopher
and close friend of Charles Merriam at the University
of Chicago. Professor-legislator Smith's joyous effort
to have a legislative council established in Illinois reflects as directly as perhaps any single incident in the
"council movement" the impact of the Chicago group of
which Merriam was the leader, and with which Henry
Toll and his successor, Frank Bane, were associated.

2. Ibid., pp. 3-5.

3. Ibid., p. 6.

4. Ibid., p. 7.

5. Illinois Revised Statutes, chapter 63, sections
33-42.

6. Ibid., section 33. This section also provides
that in no event shall the majority party in either House
be represented by more than two-thirds of the members
of the said council from either House.

7. Ibid., section.34 (2). It is worthy of note that
the Illinois legislation has been amended only twice,
each time to eliminate a termination clause, which initially provided for the lapse of the council after four

years, and then for its lapse after an additional two years. The council is now a permanent establishment.

8. Charles M. Kneier, "Illinois Legislative Council Completes its First Year," National Municipal Review, XXVIII (September, 1939), 640.

9. Interview with Mr. Jack Isakoff, Director of Research, Illinois Legislative Council, Springfield, Illinois, August 9 and 10, 1954.

10. Kneier, op. cit., pp. 641-642.

11. Ibid., For that matter, the amount was increased from $10,000 to $15,000.

12. Ibid. T. V. Smith, the first Chairman of the council, had meanwhile departed for Washington, D.C., and a seat in the House of Representatives. His influence over the creation of the organization was evidently greater than his control over its activities once it had been established.

13. "Relationships Between Council Proposals and Bills Introduced," Research Memorandum 1-226, Illinois Legislative Council, Springfield, November, 1950, pp. 1-2.

14. Isakoff interview.

15. Ibid.

16. Ibid.

17. On paper one notes a similarity to Kansas. Committees are assigned to cover agriculture, taxation, banking, education, government organization, industry and insurance, the judiciary, labor, welfare, utilities, transportation and highways; there are also four administrative committees. All are listed in the current Annual Report of the agency.

18. The caliber of the organization's research reports is conclusive testimony in support of this assertion. They are highly regarded not only in Illinois but throughout the nation, as a result of their being made available directly and through the Council of State Governments.

19. Isakoff interview. This point has been verified by correspondence with a former council employee, Dr. Richard G. Browne; letter to me dated August 23, 1954. Dr. Browne formerly served as Director of Research for the council.

20. Illinois Legislative Council, Annual Report 1952-53, p. 7. The newsletter has since become a monthly report during the period between legislative sessions.

21. Rule 6, ibid., p. 24.

22. Rule 7, ibid., pp. 24-25.

23. Rule 8, ibid., p. 25.

24. Isakoff interview.

25. Illinois Legislative Council, Annual Report 1952-53, p. 25. Rule 10.

26. Rule 9, ibid., p. 25.

27. An example of a substantially factual report is "Dram Shop Liability," Research Memorandum 1-670, November, 1952. This ten-page report discusses the tort liability imposed on sellers of alcoholic beverages by Illinois law, and summarizes the civil damage statutes of 32 other states, setting forth some of the significant similarities and differences between Illinois and these states.

28. See, for example, Structure of Governments in Metropolitan Areas, Publication 113, November, 1952; "Penalties for Escape from Penal Confinement," Research, Memorandum 1-631, July, 1952; "Current Sexual Deviate Legislation," Research Memorandum 1-634, August, 1952; "State Claims for Old-Age Pension Grants," Research Memorandum 1-642, August, 1952; "State Police Forces," Research Memorandum 1-715, January, 1953, for a few of many possible examples.

29. Illinois Legislative Council, Verification of Election Results, Publication 118, Springfield, April, 1954, p. 27.

30. Illinois Legislative Council, Annual Report 1952-53, p. 9.

31. Rule 10, op. cit., p. 25.

32. Illinois Revised Statutes, Section 40.

33. Isakoff interview.

34. "Relationship Between Council Proposals and Bills Introduced," op. cit. The following figures are from this Report, pp. 3-6.

35. Illinois Legislative Council, Annual Report 1951-52, p. 6.

36. Isakoff interview.

37. Samuel K. Gove and Gilbert Y. Steiner, The Illinois Legislative Process (Urbana, University of Illinois, Institute of Government and Public Affairs, June, 1954), p. 22. The immediately following material is largely based upon this source, pp. 22-23.

38. Ibid.

39. Rule 13, op. cit. p. 26.

40. Isakoff interview.

41. Ibid.

42. Gove and Steiner, op. cit., p. 27.

43. Ibid. The following is based upon this source, pp. 12, 27-36.

44. Ibid., p. 29.

45. Senator George Drach, majority whip, quoted in ibid., pp. 12-13.

46. Letter, R. G. Browne to author, op. cit.

47. It is somewhat more accurate to say that the Illinois council plus the Illinois Legislative Reference Bureau constitute advanced implementation of the legislative reference bureau concept, the bill-drafting function being found in the latter organization. Note, however, McCarthy's observation that informational assistance to the legislators is "the central main concept of the legislative reference department."

48. Gove and Steiner, op. cit., pp. 16-17.

49. Book of the States 1956-57, p. 120.

50. V. O. Key, American State Politics; An Introduction (New York: Alfred A. Knopf, 1956), esp. pp. 222-
226, 230-234.

51. Ibid., esp. pp. 227, 228-231.

52. Ibid., p. 228.

53. Ibid., p. 227.

54. Ibid., p. 223.

55. Ibid., p. 230. My colleague, Professor David
Derge of Indiana University, has been engaged in objective studies of legislative voting behavior in Illinois
which cast much doubt upon the commonly assumed
rural-urban split in the legislature.

56. Ibid., p. 53.

57. Ibid., pp. 76-77.

CHAPTER VIII

GOVERNOR'S COUNCIL— THE CASE OF KENTUCKY

In 1935 A. B. "Happy" Chandler was elected Governor of Kentucky. Young, flamboyant, ambitious, and supported by some able politicians and administrators, Happy proceeded to make a number of drastic changes in the staid and dreary pattern of Kentucky government. Among the innovations was a legislative council, whose fifteen members included ten legislators and five administrative officials designated by the governor.[1] The governor was also made an "honorary member" of this organization, whose purpose was described as "to screen out bad legislation."[2]

The council, with no appropriation of its own for administration, was staffed by employees borrowed from departments controlled by its executive branch members. Its undistinguished career suffered a setback in 1944, when the Republican party captured the governorship of Kentucky, the Democrats retaining control of the legislature. The council statute was promptly amended to eliminate the executive branch members, and with them went the council's staff. The moribund statute remained on the books until, 1948, when a new law was enacted creating the present Kentucky Legislative Research Commission.[3]

In 1955 A. B. "Happy" Chandler was once again elected Governor of Kentucky. No longer young, still flamboyant, with a checkered political past and an o'erweening passion to be President, Happy proceeded to make a number of drastic changes in Kentucky state government. One of his early acts was to fire the

163

director of the legislative research commission and to
replace him with Lieutenant Governor Harry Lee Waterfield, who thus became the administrative head of the
commission as well as its ex officio chairman.

The 1948 act creating the Kentucky Legislative Research commission provided that "the Governor shall
be ex officio chairman of the commission, but may for
such periods as he may determine, designate the Lieutenant Governor as a member of the commission to act
as chairman in his place."[4] Under this provision it
soon became customary for the lieutenant governor to
function as chairman.

The act had been drafted by Dr. Arthur Y. Lloyd,
with some help from Dr. Frederick Guild of Kansas and
Mr. Herbert Wiltse of the Council of State Governments.
The commission consists of seven ex officio members,
the chairman plus the president pro tem of the senate,
the speaker of the house, and the majority and minority
party leaders of each chamber. The director is required to "have had graduate training in government at
a recognized university. . . , or practical experience in
governmental administration."[5] Dr. Lloyd, first director of the commission, more than met the required
qualifications. He had been a student and a college
teacher of political science as well as Kentucky's first
public assistance administrator. He had served briefly
as commissioner of welfare, had been an intended candidate for the superintendency of public instruction and,
like many another Kentucky politician, had at one time
nurtured gubernatorial ambitions. In 1948 he was a
personal friend and political supporter of Governor
Earle C. Clements. Independently wealthy as well as
experienced, Lloyd was no typical figure in Kentucky
politics.

The Kentucky commissioners are not selected directly by the legislature, being ex officio. The governor

usually is able to influence the selection of presiding officers and majority leaders of the two houses of the assembly. He thus has much control over the Legislative Research Commission, particularly in view of his option of serving in lieu of the lieutenant governor. As for the two minority party leaders—in Kentucky the minority party seldom exercises leadership in the legislature, displaying instead a strong tendency to go along with the administration on most matters.

The role of such a commission as this is somewhat difficult to portray precisely. It reviews staff reports before these are issued, and exercises a degree of control over the research program in this fashion and by passing upon proposals for studies submitted by the director. The group meets periodically to act on an agenda submitted by the director, and its leaders serve as one means of liaison between the organization and the governor, as well as a link with the legislative.

The commission's director exercises considerable authority in determining studies to be undertaken. From time to time he also has consulted the governor about matters under consideration within his organization, and assumed responsibility for budget and program planning, as well as staffing. Appointments to be commission staff are subject to approval by the commission, and have generally been subject also to routine political clearance. At times patronage has been a factor in the selection of staff, particularly clerical employees.

In some instances members of the commission have gone beyond passive approval of the work of the staff. During a 1951 special session called to increase the level of old-age assistance benefits, the commission vetoed a staff memorandum to legislators explaining that a comparatively small increase in the state appropriation would enable a substantial rise in benefit levels because the department in charge of the program had been holding payment levels below the level for which funds had been available. Release of this information might have been embarrassing to the administration. A 1952 staff report on parimutuel taxation was also withheld for a time because of political objections.

Some members of the commission have taken their responsibility for pre-publication review of research reports quite seriously. In general, however, they have relied upon the director to exercise proper discretion and avoid incidents which might have undesirable political consequences. In Kentucky, his position has from the beginning been one requiring a combination of professional competence, political sagacity, and political acceptability—not necessarily in this order.

At the time of its establishment the Legislative Research Commission was granted the powers and duties one commonly finds assigned to legislative councils, including the right to subpoena witnesses and records. The commission was also required to "report its findings, either with or without recommendation, to the Governor of the Commonwealth, and to each member of the General Assembly at least 30 days prior to the convening of each regular session of the General Assembly."[6]

Between 1948 and 1956, the Kentucky commission thrived. From an initial amount of $ 75,000 its appropriations grew to more than a quarter million dollars for the 1955-56 biennium.[7] At this time Kentucky's appropriation for legislative services was the third largest on record.[8] During this period the scope of the Legislative Research Commission's activities grew markedly.

In 1950 a "Committee on Functions and Resources of State Government" was established in Kentucky, somewhat along the lines of the Little Hoover Commissions found in other states after World War II. The

Legislative Research Commission was assigned to perform needed research "and in general to serve as a
secretariat for the Committee."[9]

During the 1950-51 biennium the commission began
to publish a biennial Handbook for New Legislators. It also
reproduced the legislative rules as a basis for their
revision and improvement by the General Assembly,
prepared a series of informative public reports and materials concerning Kentucky government and the Kentucky legislature, began distribution of the bills and
acts of the assembly, took custody of the office facilities
and 'equipment belonging to the legislature and began
publication of an intersession newsletter for members
of the legislature.

In the following biennium, this expansionist trend
became even more marked. The state's Statute Revision Commission, formerly an independent agency, was
made part of the Legislative Research Commission.[10]
This commission was responsible for the continuous revision and publication of the Kentucky statutes and for
bill drafting assistance to legislators. The Legislative
Research Commission was also made responsible in
1954 for the preparation and publication of a daily index and digest of legislative session actions. " This
work previously had been performed by a private publisher, and dissatisfaction with the results led legislators to assign the work to the Commission."[11]

A 1954 amendment to the LRC statute also made
the organization Kentucky's Commission on Interstate
Cooperation (in which capacity it had unofficially served
in previous years), and authorized the commission to
designate persons to represent the state at the annual
conference of Commissioners on Uniform State Laws.
Finally, the 1954 legislation appeared to remove the
Legislative Research Commission from the jurisdiction
of the administrative branch of Kentucky government by

eliminating the applicability of personnel laws and regulations and by granting the commission complete freedom in arranging for the printing of its publications,
which had formerly been subject to state printing rules.

Between 1948 and 1956 the Legislative Research
Commission also issued more than forty research reports, plus a series of informational bulletins. These
were distributed to individual members of the legislature, to newspapers within the state, and to interested
private citizens and organizations on the commission's
mailing list. Some major studies were initiated by simple or joint legislative resolutions; others were undertaken by the commission on its own initiative.

The research program was not unimpressive. Studies were usually well publicized in Kentucky's leading
newspaper, the Louisville Courier-Journal, and it
sometimes seemed that this was one of the most effective ways of bringing them to the attention of legislators.

About six years after the establishment of the Legislative Research Commission, Allen M. Trout, long-time
Frankfort representative of the Courier-Journal, observed in a burst of enthusiasm that

> The General Assembly is reasserting itself
> as the third arm of State Government in Ken-
> tucky. . . . This reaffirmation of its power is
> seen best in the Legislature's development of
> the Legislative Research Commission into a
> full-scale year-around agency.
>
> L.R.C. thus becomes the Legislature's own
> arm of continuing research, revision of stat-
> utory law, bill-drafting, and between-sessions
> housekeeping. Moreover, the Legislature re-
> moved L.R.C. from control of the Executive
> Department, insofar as qualifications of
> staff, salaries, tenure and the like are con-
> cerned. L.R.C. is now subject only to con-
> trol of the legislative arm and State Con-
> stitution.[12]

Meanwhile, the commission's director was becoming a leading figure in the field of legislative service work. In 1951 he was appointed chairman of the Council of State Governments' Legislative Service Conference Committee on the Organization of Legislative Services.[13] In 1953 he was chosen president of the Legislative Service Conference. In 1954 he felt that he had no need to worry about his tenure "in regard to the effect of shifting political winds."[14] In January, 1956, the accuracy of this judgment and the discernment of the Courier-Journal's Frankfort correspondent were both challenged. The director was removed from office by Governor Chandler.

The Policy Position of the Kentucky Legislative Research Commission

In order to avoid any criticism of partiality or usurpation of legislative power the Commission has never exercised its statutory right to make recommendations to the General Assembly. Its reports have been confined to information and analysis. Interpretation of these facts in terms of a legislative program is considered a policy-making function of the General Assembly with which the staff should not interfere.[15]

"Give the Legislators the Facts, Trust Them to Make the Decisions," reads the somewhat glib but evidently appealing slogan at the beginning of many of the commission's reports. Under the circumstances one finds in Kentucky, a policy of directly submitting a legislative program would have been unwise. The commission has not spoken for the legislature so much as for the governor and his program. The legislators generally would probably be less than enthusiastic about a

program submitted to them by this seven-man ex officio
commission. There might have been ways around this
obstacle, had the commission been inclined to follow
them, such as the use of subcommittees comprised of
legislators for the study of various subjects. But the
members of the Legislative Research Commission are
men who have been chosen more for their ability to put
across a program, to balance conflicts, and to steer the
legislature, rather than to engage in program planning
of their own. This is particularly true of the majority
leaders in each house, and to some lesser extent of the
minority leaders. Finally, if there is to be a legislative
program in Kentucky, it must be the governor's program—not that of lieutenant governor serving as chairman of the Legislative Research Commission, nor of
the commission itself representing the legislature
rather than the governor. Wisdom, convenience, and
the fact that political programs are not always premised
upon rational, objective research have supported the
fact-finding, non-recommending policy adopted by the
Legislative Research Commission.

At the same time, the Legislative Research Commission has participated in a variety of policy studies
involving the formulation of explicit recommendations
for legislative action. An aura of objectivity was maintained by the commission while tangible proposals were
produced through the happy combination of commission
research studies with proposals formulated by separate
advisory committees.

For example, House Bill No. 450 of the 1950 legislative session authorized a comprehensive study of
child welfare laws.[16] Although the authorization did not
call for any advisory body, one was appointed by the
lieutenant governor, and

during hundreds of hours of meetings, the Advisory Committee on Child Welfare . . . gradually shaped its recommendations. . . . The
recommendations were the product of the
Committee's independent conclusions. They
were not subject to review or approval by the
Legislative Research Commission.

About the time the 1952 Session began, the
Commission published its report on the project, KENTUCKY YOUTH PROBLEMS—
DELINQUENCY, CHILD LABOR, AND ADOP-
TION, summarizing important results of extensive research. As a convenience to members of the General Assembly and other
interested leaders, the publication also contained a summary of the recommendations
of the Advisory Committee on Welfare. The
committee arranged for the preparation of
legislation based upon its proposals, a substantial part of which was enacted.[17]

A comparable procedure was followed during the
1952-1954 biennium in the study of a proposal for a new
medical school at the University of Kentucky. In this
instance the commission was directed by house resolution to make

. . . a careful and impartial study of the desirability and steps necessary for the establishment of a State-supported medical school
at the University of Kentucky.[18]

The resolution authorizing the study called for recommendations, so the commission established an Advisory
Committee on Medical Education comprised of five
prominent Kentucky physicians. To no one's surprise
the committee concluded that a medical school was
needed.[19]

Perhaps the most heroic use of citizen advisory
groups by the commission occurred in connection with

its studies of education and educational finance. The Committee on Functions and Resources of State Government had recommended adoption of a constitutional amendment to permit more equitable financing of common schools. Such an amendment was initiated by the 1952 General Assembly and submitted for ratification to the electorate in November, 1953.

The Kentucky Constitution has proven singularly difficult to amend. Anticipating the possibility of passage of the amendment, the Legislative Research Commission undertook further study of school finance problems which would come before the 1954 General Assembly if the amendment were approved. The study, begun with considerable reluctance, was desired by the governor as well as the state superintendent of public instruction. Recognizing that the essential element of this undertaking was not so much a matter of research as the development of public support for the constitutional amendment, the director of the Legislative Research Commission devised an arrangement under which

> local Committees were appointed in each of the State's 228 school districts. The size of the local Committees varied, the largest consisting of 77 members, with an average of 28 members in county and 17 in independent districts. Committees in 94 per cent of Kentucky school districts took an active part in the study. Though only the votes of actual Committee members are recorded in this pamphlet, more than 20,000 citizens were consulted as part of the survey, thereby reflecting a good sampling of public opinion over the state.[20]

According to a commission report the work of these committees consisted of "collecting information, making decisions, and engendering interest in education. . . ."[21] By something less than coincidence,

an unusual degree of grass roots support was developed
for the proposed amendment to Kentucky's constitution
by these committees, which almost unanimously reported in favor of improving Kentucky's common school
system and its financing.[22] The commission was so
pleased with the work of the citizen's committees that
it passed a resolution of appreciation thanking "five
thousand two hundred and twenty-five citizens" for their
services which, we are assured, would" . . . provide
the 1954 General Assembly with a vast amount of valuable data on education. . ."[23] — to say nothing of a constitutional basis for action, as the amendment was rati-
fied at the November, 1953, election.

   During the 1952-1953 biennium, the commission's
program included the following projects which were
treated as indicated.[24]

Project Title	Advisory Committees Established	Recommendations submitted to Governor & Legislature
1. Common School Education	Yes	Yes
2. Alcoholism	Yes	Yes
3. Medical Education	Yes	Yes
4. Care of the Cerebral Palsied	Yes	Yes
5. State-city Relations	No	No
6. Strip Mining in Kentucky	No	No

   In some instances the commission has not been concerned with the preparation of legislative recommendations. A 1953 state-city relations study is a case in
point. "This project was undertaken as a result of a request from the Kentucky Municipal League for a study of

home rule for Kentucky cities."[25]   Its purpose was to
help placate or defer certain demands for "home rule."
To an extent a study of cerebral palsy and facilities for
its treatment was a comparable undertaking intended as
a concession to the Kentucky Society for Crippled Child-
ren. Although recommendations were included in the
undertaking, they were received with apathy and resulted
in no immediate legislative action.

The Legislative Research Commission survived the
transition in political leadership which occurred with
the re-election of Governor Chandler. Several members of the professional staff resigned about this time
for various reasons, including lack of sympathy for the
new administration and the availability of better jobs
elsewhere. Replacements were obtained and, although
the Commission has not retained the same spotlighted
position it occupied during the administrations of governors Earle Clements and Lawrence Weatherby, it
continues its research and service functions. For the
1958 session of the legislature the commission staff
prepared a 287 page Uniform Commercial Code based
upon the model law of the National Conference of Commissioners on Uniform State Laws and the American
Law Institute. Supported by the Kentucky Bar Association
and sponsored in the assembly by a member of the
commission, the code was adopted by a legislature
whose members were in some cases quite frank about
their inability to understand it.[26]

From the record it is clear that the policy position
of the Kentucky Legislative Research Commission is
much more complex than its slightly unctuous slogan
would suggest. "The voice is indeed the voice of Jacob;
but the hands are the hands of Esau." In ostensible
policy the Kentucky commission resembles Illinois; in
practice it has at times operated more nearly along the

lines of Kansas; in essence it is unlike either of these
organizations. The Kentucky commission has been
neither politically neutral nor consistently impartial in
relation to policy questions. It has, in short, been in
the best behaviorist tradition, the product of its immediate environment.

The Setting— Kentucky, "Where Politics Are the Damndest!"

Three factors cast much light on the reasons for
the particular character of the Kentucky Legislative Research Commission— the role of the governor, the general pattern of political organization in Kentucky, and
the resultant character of the Kentucky General Assembly.

When the Governor of Kentucky is of the same political faith as the majority of the General Assembly, he
is the commonwealth's chief legislator. In few American states does one find as great a degree of legislative
leadership as that sometimes exercised by the Governor
of Kentucky. The Legislative Research Commission
was created at the behest of Governor Clements, supported by Governor Weatherby, and commandeered by
Governor Chandler. In 1958 the legislature rejected a
bill which would have eliminated executive branch representation on the commission.[27]

Governor Clements ran the legislature with a cold,
firm hand which was sometimes resented but usually
respected. Governor Weatherby was affable and
friendly, and also effective. As for Governor Chandler,
some of the liveliest examples of contemporary American political journalism describe his legislative relations:

[The 1956 General Assembly] was driven,
rather than guided, by a Governor who regarded it sometimes with annoyance, often
with amusement, always with contempt, and
it moved by fits and starts as the Governor
applied the spur. . . . It marked an unpre-
cendented humiliation of the elected legislative body by a dictatorial governor, the almost total usurpation of the legislative
authority by the executive, and an unparal-
lelled subversion of the legislative process.
Like a flock of hens, flapping and cackling at
the approach of the fox, the Assembly ran or
froze as the Governor and his errand boys directed."[28]

In 1956 the only request refused the governor by
the legislature was for a $ 200,000 appropriation for re-
novation of the governor's mansion, which had been re-
novated only two years earlier. Abetted by the Courier-
Journal, a lot of people in Kentucky developed clear-cut
negative sentiments about this simple, tangible issue.
After an unusual show of opposition in the senate the
governor dropped his request for the funds. But on
August 1, a few months after the legislative session,

Governor Chandler was notified . . . that he
has to find himself a new place to live. 'This
old house,' the Executive Mansion, came up
with a seriously dangerous case of hot wires.
An emergency was declared by Dr. James W.
Martin, finance commissioner. . . . The Governor and his family were told to be 'out'
within 60 days. . . . Martin estimated 'very
roughly' all the work planned on the mansion
would cost $ 1 75, 000 to $ 200, 000. The money
would come out of a general appropriation to
the Finance Department for buildings and maintenance.[29]

In 1958, facing his second legislature in a state where the governor cannot succeed himself, Chandler again managed to carry the field, with the exception of an attempt to rip some authority from the elected anti-Chandler Democratic state treasurer.

A number of factors help explain the power of the governor of Kentucky and his resulting legislative strength. In 1936 a reorganization established a strong governor pattern of administration, with centralized control of patronage, state finances, and administrative organization generally. The governor is in a position to reward the faithful and to punish those who fall away. A number of the legislators, for example, are, in the best American tradition, businessmen. The commonwealth buys a lot of commodities in the course of a year, and a share of this business customarily goes to loyal supporters. The legislature understandably defeated in 1958 a "conflict of interest" bill which would have barred members from entering into business contracts with the state.

The fulcrum beneath the governor's lever is the fragmented, factional character of Kentucky state politics. The commonwealth sprawls across a large and diverse area, ranging from the traditionally Republican mountain country of the east and southeast through the Bourbon Bluegrass with its Southern Democratic flavor, over a large but scattered area of tobacco and general farming, much of it relatively poor, to the western end of the state where industrial Paducah mingles with the lingering flavor of Judge Priest and the legend of Irvin S. Cobb. Finally, in the north one finds Louisville, major metropolitan area in its own right, and further up the river the Covington district of northern Kentucky, rather closely linked with the Cincinnati metropolitan region of which it is a part.

There is no true rural-urban split, for the urban

areas are without sufficient power, representation, or commonality of interest. Among the various rural regions one finds complex cleavages, some of them based on political events of fifty years or more ago. To command the state one must weld factions together within the framework of the Democratic party. There is always a degree of uneasiness and ephemerality in these amalgamations, which are put together in the long politicking months before election-time. When major rifts occur, as they do at intervals, there may be an overthrow of one faction by another, as in the 1955 defeat of the Weatherby-Clements group by Governor Chandler, or a momentary upsurge of the Republicans, which also occurred about the same time, producing two Republican U.S. Senators from Kentucky and a Republican urge to capture the governship in 1959.

In this environment, politics is personal rather than issue oriented. Control of the state trends to mean "something for everybody" who participated in the campaign. So long as the deserving get their desired desserts, the governor is relatively free to get his.[30] One further element of this picture is the presence of an array of effective interest groups, primarily interested in the protection of their own perquisites and positions. Thus, in order to obtain a new driver licensing law in 1958, providing for the central issuance of licenses by the Department of Public Safety, it was necessary to make a satisfactory settlement with the circuit court clerks who previously issued the licenses. Agreement was reached by granting the clerks a fee of seventy-five cents out of each $2.00 charged for license renewal.

This pattern of politics works its effects upon the legislature, which is not much of a policy-making body. It seldom initiates, infrequently deliberates, and usually ratifies. A considerable degree of furor and debate can be roused for such earthy and focused issues

as daylight-saving versus standard time, the licensing
of dogs, and similar matters. Yet the legislature is not
without significance. In extreme cases, stirred by a
surge of popular opinion, it can rise to echo the voice of
the public; and though this happens infrequently, it is
always an unforgettable potentiality.

Beyond this the General Assembly has two further
merits: it serves as an obstacle course through which
policy proposals must pass, subject to the keen scrutiny
of the various represented interests, and to the moderat-
ing force of balance and compromise. Even more than
this the legislative process subjects the plans and policies of the state and its leadership to publicity, making
it necessary for them to be less implausible than might
otherwise be the case, for there is often the desire to
look good, and to avoid appearing too crass or foolish;
and there is always also the threat of future public action against too-irresponsible politicians— although it
is sometimes difficult to pin as much faith as hope upon this premise.

The character of the Kentucky General Assembly
is rather well illustrated by the working of its standing
committees. The committee system is almost evanes-
cent; intensive legislative scrutiny of proposed enactments simply does not occur in committees. Practically
the only committee hearings in recent years consisted
of brief discussions of the executive budget before informal assemblages of both legislative houses. In both
1952 and 1954 the budget was enacted within the first
week of the legislative session, which suggests the extent to which it received legislative study.

"Public hearings are the exceptional practice in
committee procedure. . . ."[31]   The kindest description
of them describes committees as usually meeting "hur-
riedly in little knots in the corners of the two chambers
before the two bodies convene."[32]

> Committees do not employ any staff to keep
> minutes or make a record of testimony. . . .
> Many committees never receive a bill and
> can be conceived of as mere window-dressing
> in the legislative superstructure. Others re-
> ceive only one or two bills. A few, in contrast,
> receive the great bulk of proposed legislation.[33]

These few, especially the rules committees of the
two houses, really control the flow of legislation. The
rules committees receive all bills introduced in the final fifteen days of a session and take control of all bills
not having had a third reading by that date. About ninety
per cent of all Kentucky legislation is enacted in these
final days, and one cannot underestimate the significance
of these two committees, whose membership is generally
controlled or determined by the governor. They are primarily steering committees, not deliberative bodies.

In this setting the common attitude of legislators toward the Legislative Research Commission is one of
reasoned apathy, tempered by occasional interest in
subjects of its study or the desire for some assistance
of one kind or another. It is not their organization; they
know it, and they don't particularly care. The semi-
obscured policy work of the council is really an adjunct
of gubernatorial leadership. The commission is a research and policy-planning arm of the executive, and
this, rather than the question of whether it makes recommendations or not, is the salient key to an understanding
of the organization. Only on this basis can any adequate
assessment be made of the Kentucky Legislative Research Commission.

The Kentucky Commission—
An Appraisal

The Legislative Research Commission represents no significant adaptation of the legislative process in Kentucky; but it has made a significant contribution to policy planning and policy making.[34]   Not all of this has been on so lofty a plain as to be pleasing to the politically squeamish. Out of the not entirely impartial study of the commission has come, perhaps to the chagrin of some former members of the staff, the A. B. Chandler Medical Center, a not-unmixed blessing to the financially limited state of Kentucky. But looking back over ten years one finds also a rather impressive array of contributions, including a new juvenile court law, a public retirement system, radical modernization of school finance, regulation of strip mining, improved mental health program organization, a well managed system of law codification and annotation, a modern commercial code, and certain improvements in tax administration and policy. For these and other contributions the final credit must go to a succession of chief executives. But without the resources of the commission and its competent, productive research staff and active director, many of these things would not have come to pass. As a much-needed policy-planning staff, the commission operated as an adjunct of the policy-making center. The obscure character of its relation to the legislature is essentially a reflection of the more basic relation of chief executive and general assembly in Kentucky. The utility of the commission is suggested by the fact that Governor Chandler modified his original inclination to abolish it. It is of course true that he was not uninterested in its patronage aspect, but under his regime the organization has continued its policy studies.

In Kentucky the non-recommending feature of the Legislative Research Commission is primarily a matter of tactics. The fact that the commission makes no overt recommendations is not so significant as its rather direct role in policy planning, which is currently reflected in the neat dovetailing of the positions of commission chairman and staff director in the same person, a lieutenant governor who has also been styled "the Governor's lieutenant." This arrangement may be changed in the future, but the basic role of the commission is not likely to change, so long as the organization continues to exist.

Thus in Kentucky one finds a research-policy synthesis quite different from that of Kansas—a somewhat devious and sometimes dubious arrangement which yet meets the essential tests of need and practicality. And if the neatness and stability of the Kentucky arrangement are not so great as Kansas', this is a reflection of the environment rather than inherent flaws of organizational arrangement.

Notes

1. Gladys M. Kammerer, "The Development of a Legislative Research Arm," Journal of Politics, XII (Autumn, 1950), 654.

2. Conversation with Dr. Arthur Y. Lloyd, Director of the Kentucky Legislative Research Commission, 1948-1955, June 22, 1954.

3. Kentucky Revised Statutes, 1949, Sec. 7.090 (Chapter 15, sec. 3, Session Acts of 1948). Additional material concerning the 1936 council will be found in Gladys M. Kammerer, "Right About Face in Kentucky," National Municipal Review, XXXVII (June, 1948), 303-308; also in her "Legislative Oversight of Administration in Kentucky," Public Administration Review, X (Summer, 1950), 169-176.

4. KRS 7.090, op. cit., section 1.

5. Ibid., Sec. 3.

6. Ibid., 7.110 (italics added).

7. Book of the States 1956-57, p. 120.

8. Only Ohio's Legislative Service Commission, with $ 400,000 and Missouri's Committee on Legislative Research, with $ 300,000, exceeded Kentucky.

9. Kentucky Legislative Research Commission, Second Biennial Report (Frankfort: February, 1953), p. 7.

10. Kentucky Legislative Research Commission, Third Biennial Report, p. 2.

11. Ibid., p. 2. The following paragraph is drawn from pp. 2-3 of this report.

12. "Assembly Regains Former Eminence: Becomes Political Proving Grounds," Louisville Courier-Journal, March 21, 1954.

13. Special Committee on Organization of Legislative Services, Legislative Service Conference, Revised Preliminary Report (Council of State Governments: Chicago, September 22, 1953, offset), Foreword.

14. Lloyd conversation, op. cit.

15. Third Biennial Report, op. cit., pp. 1-2.

16. This project was originally to have been authorized by House Resolution 68 which called for establishment of an advisory committee to help plan the study and formulate recommendations. The resolution, drafted with the help of the director of the Legislative Research Commission, passed both houses but failed to become effective because it was not presented to the presiding officers for signature. It was apparently mislaid by a legislative clerk on loan from the Department of Economic Security, whose commissioner was opposed to the project.

17. Second Biennial Report, op. cit., p. 9.

18. H. R. 46, quoted in Third Biennial Report, op. cit., p. 12.

19. It is now known as the Albert B. Chandler Medical Center, at the University of Kentucky, Lexington.

20. Kentucky Legislative Research Commission, Kentucky's Education Puzzle—5,000 Citizens Report on Their Schools, informational Bulletin No. 8, Frankfort, Kentucky, August, 1953, Foreword.

21. Ibid.

22. Ibid., pp. 12-13.

23. "A Resolution of Appreciation," ibid., inside back cover.

24. The tabulation is based upon Third Biennial Report, op. cit., pp. 7-16.

25. Ibid., p. 15.

26. "How Good—Or Bad—Was the Legislature?" Louisville Courier-Journal, March 23, 1958.

27. Ibid. According to this newspaper story, ". . . the L.R.C. is under the active direction of Lieutenant Governor Harry Lee Waterfield, and is thus little more than a research arm of the Administration."

28. Louisville Courier-Journal, April 30, 1956.

29. Louisville Courier-Journal, August 2, 1956.

30. Some light is thrown on this general process of executive leadership in Kentucky by Coleman B. Ransone, Jr., The Office of Governor in the South (Tuscaloosa: University of Alabama Press, 1951), esp. pp. 74, 88-96, and 219. Highway patronage is a vital political force.

31. This splendid understatement is found in Gladys M. Kammerer, "Kentucky's Legislature Under the Spotlight," Kentucky Law Journal, XXXIX (November, 1950), 53-54.

32. Ibid., p. 53.

33. Ibid., p. 54.

34. As supervisor of research for the KLRC,

1950-1952, the author first came in contact with the
legislative service field, and formed attitudes and im-
pressions which at times make difficult the maintenance
of an attitude of austere detachment.

CHAPTER IX

A FURTHER ESSAY IN DIVERSITY

In Kansas, in Illinois, and in Kentucky there exist three distinctly different types of organizations, each labelled a legislative council or "council-type agency." The Kansas council is a legislative program-planning body; the Illinois council is essentially concerned with research and reference; the Kentucky Legislative Research Commission is a research and policy-planning adjunct of the governor's office, and to some extent a means of linking the chief legislator with the general assembly.

The general treatment one finds of American legislative councils and related agencies tends to lump them all together and to conclude that, in general, they are "good."[1] One does find distinctions between "recommending councils" and "non-recommending councils," a delineation which still assumes an identity of species.[2] One recent unpublished study refers at length to the "changing emphasis as to the role of the council," and purports to discern a general shift among legislative councils from program planning to the more limited "performance of a research and fact-finding service."[3] The record does not support the statement.[4] Rather than any trends of this sort among the councils themselves, one finds a lot of local variations on a few organizational themes. And the further one looks, the clearer are the reasons which seem to explain what exists.

Wiscons<u>in</u>: <u>A</u> <u>Council</u>
And <u>A</u> <u>Group</u> <u>of</u> <u>Legislative</u> Services

In Wisconsin "the Governor doesn't cut too much
ice."[5]   In this setting an impressive array of legislative
services has developed, centered around needs and opportunities for legislative leadership, and involving a
subtle but highly effective pattern of relationships between a long-established reference bureau and a relatively new legislative council.

The responsibility of the council is to arrive at
policy positions. The reference bureau operates on a
presumption of "complete objectivity." Yet, as its director has observed regarding recommendations, "everybody does it—you <u>have</u> to do it; the legislators demand
it."[6]   This process of making evaluations is sometimes
subtle, sometimes quite casual. "You do the study; the
legislator says 'O.K., what are the alternatives?' You
indicate what logical alternatives derive from a research
study, the legislator chooses the one he favors and says
'O.K. You draft the bill'—which in turn involves judgments."[7]

The dovetailing of the Wisconsin organizations tends
to rest upon the theory that one is for the legislator, the
other for the legislature.[8]

In Wisconsin, most bill-drafting is done by the reference bureau, although the council does some. The
reference bureau maintains the library used by both
organizations, and there appears to be an attitude of
healthy, tolerant competition between the two organizations. The Wisconsin council "developed" substantially as a secretariat for interim committees, whose
activities in a fairly recent period tended to become a
bit absurd. These absurdities included some rather extensive junketing, and some futile attempts to make
studies and recommendations."[9]

The fifteen-man legislative council resembles a
holding company for an array of legislative study committees, which in one recent year involved all but a
small number of the legislators plus a sizeable number
of lay people—to the extent of 180 individual committee
assignments.[10] Arrangements for the use of committees
are rather flexible; they may be created by the council
itself, by the legislature via statute or joint resolution,
or by some outside organization upon invitation by the
council.[11]

The Wisconsin council has had its difficulties. The
first was a marked tendency toward proliferation of projects, despite the fact that each of these must be authorized by at least one house of the legislature. At a given
moment 25 or more projects may be under consideration. Merely keeping track of all the activities going on
at a given time, arranging for hearings, providing research facilities, synthesizing the work of committees,
and publishing reports with a staff of about five people
has been enormous.[12] A 1953 amendment to the council statute reduced this burden somewhat, permitting
the council to introduce bills only upon approval by a
two-thirds vote of its membership, and cutting down the
number of council subjects in the 1955 legislature to 46
from a previous session record of over 100 bills introduced.[13] The council has also been criticized for
listening too intently to interest groups in formulating
its recommendations.[14]

The Wisconsin council has operated effectively along
the general lines of the "Kansas plan." It has broadened
and deepened the scope of legislator participation in
policy deliberations and has had its impact within the
legislature. In 1951, 72 per cent of its proposals were
enacted, amounting to 79 out of a total of 109 bills and
resolutions drafted under council auspicies.[15] The 1953
"batting average" was 61 per cent.[16] The existence of

an effective legislative reference agency in Wisconsin left no alternative for the Wisconsin council but to operate at the heart of the policy maelstrom. It attempted at one point to take over the Legislative Reference Library, but backed off with burned fingers.[17] In practice, the parallel operation of the two organizations has posed no insurmountable problems. An admitted need for more systematic legislative policy planning existed, and the Wisconsin council has become an established means of meeting it.

The political setting of the Wisconsin council is worthy of note. In Wisconsin "only in 1932 did the Democrats elect a governor in this century, and the state legislature is three-quarters Republican."[18] The Republican party has been the majority party of the state since 1938. Its cohesion tends to rest upon a relatively homogeneous general outlook of "social and economic individualism" applicable to most state and local affairs at least.[19] Admitting the presence of this general outlook, one must note also that the Wisconsin parties " seem unable to state a consistent party creed and enact a consistent program of legislation. . . . And in Wisconsin the problem of party discipline is compounded by the lingering LaFollete tradition of suspicion of strong parties and strong party leadership."[20]

In Wisconsin the political party influences the selection of political candidates; it furnishes one framework within which compromises are worked out on political issues in the context of an underlying cohesion. In other words, Wisconsin one-partyism is not a complete denial of political diversity; rather, the character and range of that diversity have not proved imcompatible with the maintenance of a stable majority group over a period of at least two decades.

The governor of Wisconsin, elected for a two-year term of office, cannot be characterized simply as "weak."

But his stay is brief; and if he cannot be substantially
controlled by his party once in office, neither can he
use the party mechanism as a potent means for dominat-
ing the legislature. Legally, he possesses a rather high
degree of financial control over the administration of
the state's services.[21] His opportunities for exercising
it vary, however. Certainly he does not dominate the
legislature. And that legislature remains imbued with
some of the questing activism of the "Wisconsin tradition." Wisconsin legislators do not limit their activities
to the times of nomination and election and to the final
days of a legislative session. Extensive use of interim
commissions preceded the Wisconsin Legislative Council.

In short, in Wisconsin one finds political homogeneity reflected in the legislature and in executive–legislative relations. One also finds an absence of effective,
persistent gubernatorial control of the legislature, an underlying tradition of staff assistance to the legislature, many
of those members have a political outlook of "enlightened
conservatism," plus an unquestioned acceptance of a
positive role for the legislature in making policy. In
Wisconsin, the legislative council is a logical extension
of a pattern of legislative services which goes back to
the turn of the century, and it reflects something of the
modern-day continuation of a frontier philosophy of government and representation.

In its essential aims and processes the Wisconsin
council resembles the Kansas council, with some modification in structure and method. But if Wisconsin reflects some adaptation of the idea of the legislative
council to local circumstances it also exemplifies the
applicability of the council arrangement to a particular
type of political setting.

Indiana

Looking elsewhere, one finds a succession of examples of diversity in the forms and functions of organizations which have been collectively treated as legislative councils. Indiana is another case in point. The 1945 legislature created a Legislative Advisory Commission "to assist the general assembly . . . in the proper performance of its constitutional functions by providing its members with impartial and accurate information and reports concerning the legislative problems which come before them,"[22] and to prepare policy proposals.[23] It has been designated by the Council of State Governments as an agency recommending to the legislature "a substantive legislative program."[24] In reality it has never functioned except as a device by which a lieutenant governor (its statutory chairman) drew additional public attention to his persistent and successful campaign for the governship between 1952 through 1956. The staff of the Indiana Legislative Advisory Commission has consisted of the almost inactive Indiana Legislative Bureau mentioned previously in this volume.

In 1955 the Indiana legislature appointed an interim committee to investigate the wisdom of establishing a legislative council.[25] Its deliberations were inconclusive. Whether there exists in Indiana a sufficient basis in need and acceptance for a positive approach to legislative leadership within the legislature remains to be seen.

This examination of a few representative specimens of the legislative council supports one conclusion: we may speak of the legislative council in abstract, but the actual organizations to which the term has been applied vary considerably in their essential characteristics. A useful single concept of "the legislative council" cannot

be applied with great precision to all of the organizations which have been labelled councils. The Kansas
Legislative Council and the Illinois Legislative Council
for example represent almost two antipodal "ideal types."

Structural Characteristics of Legislative Councils and Related Agencies

Detailed information concerning the general structure of organization found in American legislative councils and research agencies is available in the Book of
the States.[26] The record shows variations in the size,
in appropriations, and in functions.

Size of the Legislative Group

One of the most evident variations in size. Councils and research committees range from all the members of the legislature in three states—Oklahoma, Nebraska, and South Dakota—to as few as five members in
South Carolina.[27] Typical agencies have from 12 to 27
members. The question of size has been discussed in
terms of the advantage of small versus large organizations, but only limited generalizations can be made.
These advantages may be obtained through use of a
larger number of members: a degree of continuity from
session to session in the face of legislative turnover, a
chance for more diverse representation of interests,
and a greater degree of legislator participation (including more persons to help with the work). To some extent, too, a larger body might in some instances mini-
mize opposition to "domination by a little legislature."

One problem of legislative program councils is that
of continuity. Members of the legislature are elected
not at the beginning of a council's interim operations,
but near the end of them. The presence of council

members in the legislature in the session following the
period of study is not unimportant to a program council,
as the study of Kansas indicates.

The matter of council size can be approached in
two ways: in terms of an organization to serve as <u>the</u>
joint interim group of legislators, with no additional representation, or in terms of a combination of a council
plus subcommittees or advisory committees drawn from
noncouncil members of the legislature (and even from
outside the legislature). Kansas, with its rather large
(27 member) council represents one approach. Wisconsin, with 15 council members and a total of more than a
hundred committee assignments, represents another. In
a state with a tradition of extensive interim committee
assignments the latter arrangement might be more de-
sirable.

For the "non-program council" or legislative research agency the size of the legislative committee is
not so important, except as it may tend to strengthen
the relationship between the research product and the
legislature.

Finally, it is possible for any of these organizations
to become too large for effective functioning. The Oklahoma council, with its 165 members, is not fundamentally different than before its membership was enlarged,
except perhaps in the minds of the legislators. It is
operated by a relatively small executive committee.
In three other states—Nebraska, Pennsylvania and
South Dakota—all legislators are also members of the
Legislative council.

Essentially, any council may be viewed as a joint
interim committee. As an operating entity it is bound
to be smaller than the total legislature (with the exception of the relatively small Nebraska assembly, whose
43 members do meet and deliberate as a council prior
to the beginning of a legislative session, reviewing the

proposals prepared by council subcommittees.)[28] Local
considerations about representation of particular factions, areas, and the minority party will influence the
size of a council. The desirability of a degree of continuity in its membership is also likely to affect its
composition.

The Research Staffs

In the staffing arrangements of legislative councils
one finds considerable variation among the states. An
important element of any legislative council or research
agency is a competent research staff selected and per-
mitted to work without political interference. An organization can acquire a competent staff on a partisan
basis, and a substantial and explicit lack of sympathy toward the local political atmosphere would hardly en-
hance the value of a research staff member, but a staff
untouched by political pressures is probably a prere-
quisite to the lasting maintenance of an aura of objectivity. It appears that patronage pressures have posed no
problems for most legislative councils.

The size of council research staffs varies considerably from state to state, ranging from as few as two or
three professional staff members to as many as about
20 in Pennsylvania. Research staffs of existing agencies
appear to be made up predominantly of persons with two
types of training, — law or political science, although one
also finds occasional accountants, journalists, and products of other fields of academic study.[29] A preference
of persons with rather broad backgrounds has been
noted.[30]

Council research staffs appear to be rather stable,
despite the fact that they are covered by merit system
provisions in only a few exceptional cases. Most council directors remain with their organizations for long
periods of time.[31] Turnover among subordinate staff

members is somewhat higher, and is probably influenced
by salaries, which tend to be relatively low in relation
to available alternative employment, with annual wages
of $ 5,000 or less predominating in recent years.[32]

If there is one critical factor in legislative council
and research agency staffing, it is of course the choice
of a director. The significance of personalities in council operations cannot be underestimated, and the ability
and attitude of the director, executive secretary, or director of research seems vital. The role he chooses
to play is likely to have a profound effect upon the organization. Not only can he wreck it through ineptness
or imperception; his positive approach will tend to set
limits upon the agency's development.

Nebraska is a case in point. One of the oldest councils, created in the heady atmosphere of a novel experiment in legislative organization, regarded as a vital element of the unicameral legislature, operating in the
context of weak gubernatorial leadership, it was marked
between 1937 and 1953 by a relatively undistinguished
performance, largely as a result of the approach taken
by its late director.[33]

He ran the Nebraska council with a shoe-string
staff. He retained his professorship at the University of
Nebraska on a half-time basis, meanwhile administer-
ing the work of the council and undertaking most of its
research studies with the help of three clerks, a budget
analyst, and a part-time research assistant.

Until recently tne Nebraska council operated as a
program agency in low gear. One significant and surprising weakness in its customary process seems clear:
the linking of council action to the legislative process
has been relatively vague. It has been

> traditionally incumbent upon no one to take up
> the espousal of council proposals in the legis-
> lature, and it is not uncommon for the chairman

or members of council committees to fail to
take any action to support in the legislature
proposals formulated by their own committees and approved by the council.[34]

Although its legislator-members receive no pay
other than mileage and expenses for council work, they
appear to have been consistently interested in the council—to the extent of expanding its membership to include all 43 members of the Nebraska legislature in
1941. Each legislator serves upon at least one council
committee. Until about 1953, ten research studies were
perhaps representative of the council's intersession
workload, although the number of assignments appears
to have doubled since that time.

The past position of the Nebraska council was not
exactly one of strong legislative leadership. The pattern established by the council was a source of chagrin
to Professor Senning, who in the mid—1930's had visualized it as a central element in the unicameral legislature, and potentially the most effective organization of
its sort in the United States. Its further development
under a new director is being felt, but in the face of the
precedent of almost twenty years plus one of the most
stable state legislatures in the United States, radical
change will not come rapidly in Nebraska.[35]

Legal Status of Legislative Policy Agencies

Another facet of the legislative councils and research agencies which deserves some notice is their legal status in the fabric of government. With the exception of the Montana case of State ex rel. Mitchell v.
Holmes,[36] the constitutionality of the organizations has
not been successfully challenged. In Montana it appeared for a time that all interim committees were unconstitutional as a consequence of the ruling in the

above-cited case, which was brought in 1954 by a group
of Democrats after a change of administration placed Republicans in control of both governship and legislature.
This had led to the appointment of three interim committees, one of which was to investigate state construction
contracts let by the previous Democratic administration.
This in turn produced the abolition of the committees and
the legislative council via the circuitous route of judicial
interpretation. In 1957, however, a legislative council was
again established in Montana, and its constitutionality
was upheld by the Montana supreme court.[37]

To some extent, the Mitchell case concerned the
application of particular sections of the Montana constitution. At the same time, on some points it went
against the grain of a series of previous judicial decisions and attorneys' general rulings in various American states, all of which have upheld the constitutionality
of legislative councils and interim committees.[38] The
legitimacy of councils and research organizations has
been based upon the authority of the legislature to conduct investigations, to establish committees—including
interim committees—and to create organizations and
appropriate funds for public purposes.

The first question of constitutionality arose in Oklahoma in 1937. It dealt with the proposal for payment of
compensation to legislative council members, and was
readily resolved by the attorney general in favor of the
proposed legislative council arrangement.[39] The legislative council viewed constitutionally "appears to be a
simple adjunct to the legislature created for the purpose of assembling information, submitting reports,
and performing other service functions which assist
the legislative process."[40]

Apparently the position of legislative council staffs,
such as research departments, in our tripartite pattern of government has not been the subject of

constitutional questions in the courts. Some council and
research agency staffs are treated as units of the executive branch, at least for some purposes. The Illinois
Legislative Council staff is subject to the executive budget process and specifically exempted from state personnel laws and regulations which, by inference, would
otherwise apply. The Kentucky commission has been
specifically excluded from statutory requirements applicable to administrative agencies. Answers to the
question whether legislative service agency staffs are
technically in the executive or legislative branch of a
given government will vary from state to state. The
question seems to have been seldom raised, and the answers appear to have little functional significance.

The Range of Legislative Agency Functions

One further general characteristic of the councils
and research agencies merits attention: the range of
their functions. The legislative reference bureaus were
originally created for two purposes — research and bill
drafting. The program councils have been assigned the
task of formulating legislative proposals, which has included by implication the duty of legislative oversight
of administration. This study has been intentionally
circumscribed to exclude consideration of a host of
technical staff services to state legislatures in an effort to focus upon policy staff assistance. In some
places, however, the functions of policy staff organizations have been growing to encompass a variety of
housekeeping activities for the legislatures and their
members, causing some policy staff organizations to
come to resemble complex legislative secretariats.

To generalize about this trend is difficult, for the
developments have taken place in various ways in various places, and in some of them not at all. One will recall that many of the earlier legislative reference bureaus

shrivelled into bill-drafting agencies and little more.
With some risk of overstatement one can say that current trends among legislative councils and research organizations appear to move in the opposite direction, as
policy staffs acquire additional functions without sacri-
ficing their primary aims and efforts. Perhaps this ac-
cretion of function, to the extent that it is taking place,
can be explained by the fact that the newer councils and
research agencies are closer to the legislatures and
legislators than were the legislative reference bureaus
—and to the fact that the needs of the legislatures have
grown with the passing years.

One significant growth of legislative service agency
functions has been in budgetary review and/or post-
audit. For two decades the Nebraska council has done a
thoroughly satisfactory job of budget analysis and review.

Perhaps the highest form of development in this
general area of expanding and integrating legislative
services is represented by the Ohio Legislative Service
Commission, created in 1953 to integrate reference
work, statute revision, legislative programming, and
continuous fiscal review of state operations.[41] This
agency, which replaces a council-type organization, the
Ohio Program Commission, is too new to merit anything like a final assessment, but during the Lausche administration it appeared to be a dynamic focal point for
legislative programming plus administrative and fiscal
oversight in Ohio.[42] Working in the context of a sharp
cleavage between legislature and governor plus the lack
of integrated or intensive gubernatorial direction of the
executive branch, the Ohio Legislative Service Commission, whose director has a background of legal training
and political activity in Ohio, quickly developed into a
dominant legislative force. Whether it will establish a

firm foundation in the shifting and sometimes treacher-
ous sands of its setting remains to be seen.

In 1954 the state of New Jersey also created an integrated legislative service agency, the Law Revision
and Legislative Services Commission, to link budget
review, legislative research and statute revision functions.[43]   This organization, however, has no responsibilities for legislative programming.

Currently California has the most comprehensive
array of legislative service organizations, including a
legislative counsel, administrative-legislative reference
service, legislative budget committee, law revision commission, and a legislative audit committee and bureau.[44]
The California organization of legislative services,
which does not include a legislative council, is characterized by its lack of structural integration.

To tally up, one finds varied combinations of duties
and services in the legislative councils and research
agencies of American state legislatures. No single pattern of service organization predominates, but the general trend seems to be toward the expansion of legislative services in ways appropriate to the circumstances
of individual states. Twelve legislative councils or research agencies now engage in the continuous study of
state revenues and expenditures as part of their assignments.[45]   (In about the same number of states, separate
legislative organizations exist, with one or more permanent staff members, to do work of this type.) Eight
legislative councils and research organizations are
responsible for analysis of the state budget and for assistance to legislative budget committees during and
between sessions. (In 13 states this work is done by
other permanent legislative organizations.) At least
four legislative policy staffs are responsible for legislative post-audits. Five councils (including Kentucky)
and several research agencies are assigned the task of

statute revision. Currently, only nine of the 21 program
planning councils are limited in their duties to the specific tasks of research, reference and legislative programming, and in nearly all of these states other agencies exist to perform technical and housekeeping
services for the legislature.[46]

   In 1951 the Legislative Service Conference of the
Council of State Governments began a continuing study
of this entire question of legislative organization.[47]
While it has understandably come forth with no sweeping recommendations, it has looked with some favor toward the integration of legislative services.[48] And in
all probability one trend among the American state legislatures will continue to be a noticeable expansion of
legislative service activities as outgrowths of mounting
needs and service effectively rendered by existing organizations.

   In the field of fiscal review and analysis such a development may in some states represent a significant
extention of the council and research agency concepts.
Legislative oversight of administration is, after all, in-
separable from the shaping and modification of policies
to be implemented by administrative means.

   This writer's limited experience includes at least
one instance in which an elaborate planning effort led
to the legislative creation of an organization to imple-
ment a broad program which was quietly and effectively
obliterated in the course of its administration. The
legislature never knew what was happening.

   Our part-time citizen legislators lack the resources
with which to penetrate the administrative maze, save
in the most extreme instances involving special legislative investigations. Under our tripartite plan of state
government, there exists in theory at least a legislative
responsibility for review and evaluation of the work of
administration. Some of this can be done through the

use of legislative research and legislative council-type
agencies. And one of the most effective media for such
an effort is the continuing review and analysis of the
fiscal aspects of government.

The fiscal and budgetary problems of the legislatures, for that matter, document the basic trend of the
legislature's status in American state government; and
the critical inadequacy of appropriate information which
has hampered legislative budgetary control is but one
reflection of the need for assimilation and analysis of
data which has spurred the rise of the legislative reference agencies and their successors.

> . . . the problem of legislative control over fi-
> nances for many years presented no grave prob-
> lems. In fact, until three or four decades ago,
> legislative bodies assumed full responsibility
> for financial planning and policy determina-
> tion. Government was simple and relatively
> small. Taxes were very moderate, revenues
> from an expanding economy were ample, and
> costs were low. With the development of the
> executive budget system and the emergence
> of "big government" in the twentieth century,
> all this has been changed. The extensive ex-
> pansion of existing services and the constant
> addition of new governmental programs has
> transformed government into "big business."
> Budgets have become complicated, and call
> for ever increasing expenditures. Legisla-
> tors were—and still are—dismayed, torn
> between the desire on the one hand to keep
> taxes down, and the necessity on the other of
> providing funds. . .

> The problem of legislators is aggravated by
> the fact that they seldom have at their dis-
> posal the facts essential to intelligent judg-
> ment on budgetary matters. Ever suspicious
> of the executive, they fear that something is
> being "put over" on them. Yet, ordinarily,
> they dare not assume the responsibility for

> making heavy cuts in the absence of depend-
> able factual data. . .
>
> Faced with this urgent problem, legislators
> everywhere. . . have been groping for help.
> At the State level, California led off by es--
> tablishing the office of the Legislative Audi-
> tor in 1941. . . .[49]

In several other states, budget analysis has been integrated with the other work of legislative program or
legislative research agencies. Theoretically a distinct
advantage may lie in the integration of fiscal analysis
with the work of a program council, for budgetary policy
is but one aspect of many governmental policies. Fiscal policy decisions often determine the true scope and
meaning of program proposals.

There might be an inconsistency in extensive budget review and evaluation by a legislative research
agency which does not make recommendations; yet such
arrangements appear to exist. The Minnesota Legislative Research Committee affords a good illustration of
the legislative watchdog in action. This organization,
which is not a legislative program council, operates in
the context of a non-partisan legislature and considerable variation between strong and weak governors. According to its director,

> the Minnesota legislature is significantly in-
> fluenced by its non-partisan character. This
> tends to increase the feelings of 'individuality'
> on the part of the individual legislators, and
> tends to create problems of leadership not
> found to the same degree in other states where
> party organization functions.[50]

The Minnesota committee makes no recommendations, conducts no hearings, and concentrates upon the
production of research. The role of administrative

watchdog is stressed.[51]   A key function is the continuous study of state finances, including the review and
analysis of the state budget.

At the time the Minnesota organization was created
pronounced opposition to a full-fledged council sprang
up in the senate, apparently based upon fear of creating
a "little legislature."[52]   In Minnesota, "insofar as we
have legislative leadership, it comes from the governor."[53]   Meanwhile, the Minnesota Legislative Research
Committee is regarded by a number of students of Minnesota state government as failing to fill a need for a
full-fledged legislative council.   But the absence of pressure for a council is perhaps best indicated by Minnesota's "Little Hoover Commission," which in 1950 made
a number of proposals for strengthening the legislature
through the expansion of legislative services; it avoided
any suggestion that the legislative research committee
be developed into a program council.[54]

Councils and Executive-Legislative Relations

One final structural aspect of the legislative councils and research organizations remains to be discussed:
their involvement in the linking of legislative and executive contributions to the task of policy making. A strong
program council does not seem consistent with potent
gubernatorial policy leadership. Legislative research
agencies in such states as Wisconsin, Illinois, and Minnesota appear to contribute little to the deliberately
structured coordination of executive-legislative relations in the shaping of policy proposals — although this
is not true of Kentucky and Virginia, where the legislative service agencies are in reality gubernatorial controlled.

According to the Council of State Governments,
"Councils provide machinery for effective legislative
partnership with the executive in the formulation of

policy."[55] The implication that councils and research
agencies foster the coordination of efforts by the executive and legislative branches is somewhat misleading.
As a description of certain council operations it is,
however, true. The Utah council, with its gubernatorial
representative, the Arkansas council, with its legislator named by the governor to represent him, and the
New Hampshire council, with its three governor—appointed citizen members, tend as a result of their organization patterns to provide a degree of executive-
legislative coordination.[56] To even a greater extent a
less formal synthesis occurs at particular times and
places as a result of the unifying effect of politics and
policy issues which produce the same policy goals for
both chief executive and legislative leadership. But
this is the consequence of a coincidence of interests
rather than any deliberate effort to integrate executive
and legislative operations.

   Arkansas and New Hampshire are certainly characterized by a lack of deep and persistent political differences between executive and legislative branches.[57]
Any discussion of the political setting of the Utah legislative council must take account of an unusual set of
conditions including a Mormon tradition, a lively politics
conducted on a high plane, and other factors which add
up to a rather unique and distinctive context. To the
extent that a generalization can be supported, however,
it appears that most legislative program councils operate in settings characterized by a relative lack of any
continuing executive-legislative policy synthesis. Certainly no sweeping generalization about the contribution
of legislative councils to the coordinated policy making
efforts of the executive and legislative branches can be
made except as it begins and ends with an acknowledgement that the character of councils and other legislative
policy staffs and their functions are greatly shaped by

their settings—and that as these settings vary from state
to state, so will the organizations and their contributions.

Notes

1. See, for example, Graves, State Government,
op. cit., p. 261; and Zeller, op. cit., p. 139.

2. See: Harold W. Davey, "The Legislative Council
Movement, 1933-53," American Political Science Review, XLVII (September, 1953), 785-797.

3. David W. Smith, "The Legislative Council Movement in the United States" (Unpublished dissertation,
University of Utah, March, 1955), pp. 74-79.

4. Other studies which tend to treat a varied collection
of legislative staff agencies as coming within the general
category of legislative councils include Allen R. Richards,
Legislative Services with Special Emphasis on the Problems of New Mexico (Alberquerque: University of New
Mexico, 1953); Lawrence W. O'Rourke, Legislative Assistance, Some Staff Services Provided for Legislatures
(Los Angeles: Bureau of Government Research, University of California, 1951); and the Council of State Governments' Book of the States 1955-1956. See, for example, pp.
120-121, and p. 118, where it is noted that "Many councils
formulate legislative programs based on their interim research." The implication is that others don't.

5. Interview with M. G. Toepel, Chief, Wisconsin
Legislative Reference Library, August 12, 1954.

6. Ibid.

7. Ibid.

8. "The council is essentially the organization of
the legislature rather than the individual legislator."
Interview with Mr. Earl Sachse, Executive Secretary,
Wisconsin Legislative Council, August 13, 1954. "The
legislative council serves the legislature; the legislative
reference bureau works for the individual legislator."
Toepel interview.

9. Toepel interview. Pressure for creation of the

Wisconsin council appears to have stemmed in part
from newspaper critism of the interim committee situation, which led to a council proposal by State Senator G.
W. Buchen of Sheboygan in the 1947 legislature. It received wide newspaper support. See: Green Bay Press-
Gazette, March 24, 1945; Wisconsin State Journal, April
5, 1946; Appleton Post-Crescent, April 3, 1947, July 5,
1947; and the Green Bay Press-Gazette, July 24, 1947.

10. Sachse interview.

11. Ibid. In 1954 there were two council committees comprised of legislative members appointed by
the council plus "public members" appointed by the governor.

12. Public criticism has been voiced on this score.
See the Milwaukee Journal, October 17, 1949; Wisconsin State Journal, September 16, 1949.

13. "About the Legislatures," State Government,
July, 1955, p. 169.

14. See, for example, Wisconsin State Journal,
June 18, 1953; Green Bay Press-Gazette, December 19,
1950; Milwaukee Journal, October 18, 1950.

15. Madison Capital Times, January 28, 1952.

16. Sachse interview.

17. Wisconsin Legislative Council Committee on
Departmental Administration, "Reorganization Plan
Number One," Madison, November 8, 1949. (Mimeo-
graphed.)

18. Frank J. Sorauf, "Extra-Legal Political Parties in Wisconsin," American Political Science Review,
XLVII (September, 1954), 696.

19. Ibid., p. 702. Sorauf suggests the tendency toward a breakdown of this cohesive outlook in the face of
such issues as foreign policy, legislative reapportionment, and prohibition. To briefly characterize Wisconsin as a one-party state is to skim lightly over a fas-
cinating chapter of American social and political history.
To assert a tendency toward a homogeneous outlook upon the part of a politically dominant group is likewise to

paint with a broad brush indeed. For our immediate purposes, however, these brief, general observations suffice.

20. _Ibid._, p. 703.

21. Graves, State Government, pp. 370, 372, 378.

22. Laws of the State of Indiana, 84th Indiana General Assembly, 1945, Ch. 88, section 3(a).

23. _Ibid._, section 3(d) authorizes the preparation of measures for consideration by the General Assembly.

24. Book of the States 1956-57, p. 123.

25. "About the Legislatures," State Government, July, 1955, p. 186.

26. See, for example, the Book of the States 1958-59, pp. 61-71.

27. Book of the States 1955-56, p. 120

28. Jack W. Rodgers, "Assistance for the State Legislature," American Bar Association Journal, XLII (November, 1956), 1088.

29. Information on 56 research assistants cited by Smith, op. cit., indicated that more than 20 had law degrees, and another twenty had M.A.'s; 31 had prior government experience (pp. 165-168). See also O'Rourke, op. cit., pp. 14-16; Davey, op. cit., p. 788; and Kammerer, "Development of a Legislative Research Arm," op. cit., p. 656.

30. Smith, op. cit., pp. 172-173.

31. _Ibid._, p. 166.

32. _Ibid._, p. 169.

33. The following is based generally upon interviews with Dr. Jack Rodgers, who succeeded the initial incumbent of the council directorship, and with Professor Emeritus John P. Senning, one of the staunch proponents of the Nebraska unicameral literature, at Lincoln, Nebraska, August 25, 1954, and a review of publications of the Nebraska council.

34. Rodgers interview.

35. In 1954 one of its members had served con-
tinuously since 1933. Nebraska, incidentally, is another
of those politically homogeneous one party states. Technically its legislature is selected on a non-partisan ballot, but for practical purposes the state falls into a general category with Kansas, Iowa, and South Dakota in its
persistent preponderance of Republican strength, and in
such things as the relative absence of a potent urban-
rural political split. (Key, op. cit., pp. 243-246.)

36. 274 P.2nd 611 (Montana, 1954). This decision
was later overruled in State ex rel James v. Arouson
(Montana, 1957).

37. This case and the general question of the legal
status of legislative councils is discussed in David W.
Smith, "The Constitutionality of Legislative Councils,"
Western Political Quarterly, VIII (March, 1955), 68-81.
This discussion is generally drawn from the Smith article. A note on the recent reestablishment of the Montana council will be found in the Book of the States 1958-
59, at pp. 70-71.

38. The pertinent cases and rulings are cited by
Smith, ibid., pp. 69-72, 74, 76-79.

39. Ibid., p. 77.

40. Ibid., p. 75.

41. See: Book of the States 1956-57, pp. 118,
126. Also, "An Act to Create the Ohio Legislative Service Commission. . . . ," Amended Senate Bill No. 76,
enacted May 25, 1953.

42. Interview with John A. Skipton, Director, February 21, 1956. After Governor Lausche's successful
bid for a seat in the U.S. Senate, Skipton became Director of Finance in the new administration. In anticipation
of Mr. Lausche's removal from the Ohio scene, he had
been building a staff in the Ohio Legislative Service Commission from whom have been selected a number of oc-
cupants of key administrative posts in the state's executive branch.

43. Book of the States 1956-57, pp. 118-125.

44. Ibid., p. 122.

45. This and the following are based upon Book of the States 1958-59, pp. 61-69.

46. Maryland, Nevada, New Hampshire, South Dakota, Utah, Virginia, Washington, Wisconsin, and Wyoming.

47. The preliminary report of its Special Committee on Organization of Legislative Services was issued in September, 1953.

48. Revised Preliminary Report, op. cit., 8-19.

49. Graves, State Government, p. 275.

50. Interview with Mr. Louis C. Dorweiler, Director, Research Department, Minnesota Legislative Research Committee, August 19, 1954. A similar point was made by Professor Lloyd M. Short in an interview, August 20, 1954.

51. This emphasis upon oversight of administration has been explained in terms of the background and inclinations of its director, plus a widespread concern with "economy and efficiency" throughout the state. Short interview.

52. Dorweiler and Lloyd interviews.

53. Short interview.

54. How to Achieve Greater Efficiency and Economy in Minnesota's Government, Recommendations of the Minnesota Efficiency in Government Commission, St. Paul, December, 1950; esp. pp. 4, 6, 17-19.

55. Book of the States 1950-51, p. 125.

56. Book of the States 1956-57, p. 120.

57. According to Key, op. cit., p. 55, undivided party control of the governships and legislatures of these two states existed without interruption between 1931 and 1952.

CHAPTER X

CONCLUSIONS

*****

> Were our knowledge of state politics more com-
> plete, the diversity of practice would probably
> seem even more astonishing than it now appears.[1]

The diversity of American state politics has clearly
worked its effects upon what some have called "the legislative council movement." Within the shifting spectrum
of the states we now find legislative program staffs as
well as other types of organizations commonly regarded
as—and sometimes titled—legislative councils. Granting their significant differences, these organizations
share one thing in common: all are engaged in helping
plan policy, either through program planning or the more
limited work of legislative research. With a few exceptions, they are products of a development which began
(after certain preliminaries) with the establishment of
the Kansas Legislative Council.

The Requisites of the Legislative Council

The spread of state legislative policy staffs during
the past twenty-five years has not truly been a "legislative council movement," for quite a few of the organizations it has produced are not legislative councils. The
essence of the legislative council is not research but
the synthesis of technical studies and political judgments in legislative policy proposals.

What seems to be clear now is that, while research or fact finding is of value of itself alone,
if the material is to be available at the opening
of the session in a form adapted to immediate
legislative use, then research must be screened
and processed in connection with actively working legislative committees. The fact-finding
accomplishment is important, but the dividends
from the combination are far greater.

. . . active legislative participation through council membership, consequently, actually makes
research more valuable and timely, and its results more immediate.[2]

More than a third of the "legislative councils and
council-type agencies" in the United States are essentially research and reference agencies, often busily and
effectively engaged in a type of service which first began half a century ago, and—a bit ironically—in some
states working side by side with nominal legislative reference organizations which have withered into bill-
drafting agencies.

These modern research agencies incorporate certain improvements over the earlier legislative reference
bureaus. Their relationships with the legislatures are
closer and more complex. The earlier bureaus were
often tucked in a corner of the capitol, and usually af-
filiated with some administrative unit of government
such as the state library.[3] The newer legislative research agencies are under the direction and control of
legislative committees varying in size from five members in South Carolina and six in Massachusetts to about
20 in several other states.

Compared with a program planning council, legislative participation in the work of a research organization is admittedly limited, but it does exist in varying
degrees. Supervisory committees invariably participate
in the determination of subjects to be studied, which helps

relate research to anticipated legislative activity. In
addition, at least a part of the research product is directed to the legislature at large, rather than to just one
or a few of its members. In the newer research organizations such as the Illinois Legislative Council important topics of anticipated legislative deliberation receive
careful and extensive treatment.[4]

Finally, these organizations benefit in ways significant although unmeasurable from two notable developments of the past quarter-century: the spread of professional training in the social sciences which has
contributed to the quality of research, and the emergence
of coordinating and "back-stopping" facilities, particularly the Council of State Governments.

Yet there remains an essential difference between
legislative research organizations and legislative councils which cannot properly be ignored. There are no
"non-recommending councils." The difference between
legislative research and legislative program planning is
more than a matter of degree. An effective program
planning council represents a significant modification of
the legislative process; an effective research organization more nearly seeks to strengthen the traditional pattern. A council becomes a part of what Truman calls
"the group life of the legislature."[5] The true legislative council is the nearest thing to the fulfillment of
John Stuart Mill's idealized conception of the legislature
which we have known in America.

The distinction between councils and research organizations is important in part because it furnishes
clues to the environmental requisites of the program
planning council. An admittedly limited review of
American experience suggests that there are conditions
under which it is impossible for a legislative council
to operate. These can be stated as hypotheses, apparently valid but open to further investigation:

1. Great and persistent tension within the legislature, as in Illinois, or a splintered body politic leading to much "trading and dealing" in the best Kentucky fashion do not furnish adequate environments for legislative councils. In the face of deep and persistent political cleavage within the legislature the delicate synthesizing process of the council does not seem to work. In such cases one must do as in Illinois and a number of other states, where the legislative policy staff operates in a relatively detached fashion, furnishing legislative research services but avoiding policy recommendations.

2. The prospects for success of a legislative council appear inversely related to the power of the governor as legislative leader. With persistently strong executive leadership a council is likely to succumb to potent opposition, as in Michigan, or to be pulled into the executive orbit, as in Kentucky and Virginia.

> Those members of the legislature who with governors, governor-nominees, party leaders, and others seek to plan and place before the legislature policy programs with high priorities see policy-proposing legislative councils as threats to their system. . . .[6]

An effective council does pose a threat to other policy proponents, particularly to the governor who would be legislative leader. Where those who are threatened are also strong, a legislative council has little lasting prospects for survival. The authority of a council is not the authority of power, but of confidence. Councils cannot wage political warfare over any period of time with much chance of success. A council seeks to formulate a policy program without any intrinsic resources for mobilizing support and suppressing opposition through the accepted practices of the political market-place. It has no patronage, and small power to coerce (except the occasional

threat of public exposure of evident evil). A council is
akin to the "good money" of Gresham's law.

3. To be established a council requires—at least
initially—political support from outside the legislature
as well as within it. To survive, as we have noted,
there must be freedom from persistent, powerful political attack.

Professor Harold W. Davey of Iowa State College
and the leadership of the Iowa League of Women Voters
worked steadily for more than seven years for the creation of an Iowa legislative council. Davey observed that
until 1954, "No organization with sufficient political
power would support the effort."[7] Furthermore, the
dominant interest group in the state, the Iowa Farm
Bureau Federation, was "actively opposed" to a proposed agency which might threaten its own influence.
Meanwhile the legislature continued to spend considerable sums on interim committees. In 1954 both Iowa
parties officially endorsed the establishment of a legislative council, and in the following year the legislature
created not a council but a research bureau, to draft
bills, to serve as a secretariat for legislative committees, and to undertake research when formally requested
by five or more legislators. No specific appropriation
was made, but the bureau was authorized to expend
money from the state contingency fund.[8]

The number of states in which it seems feasible to
establish viable legislative councils is indeed limited.
For that matter, evolving social and economic changes
and their political consequences may in future years
threaten the continued existence of councils in some of
the states where they now exist.

The true program councils, now active in about
twenty states, represent the highest form of policy staff
organization which has emerged among the American
state legislatures. The extent to which they fulfill their

aims admittedly varies, but at their best they contribute
a great amount of systematic planning and cohesive
policy leadership. The politically neat, homogeneous,
and weak-governored states within which they can operate are a minority, and possibly a shrinking one at
that. One cannot argue wisely and well that the continued
spread of legislative councils is either likely or essential to the effective functioning of the states. The policy-
administration dichotomy which would furnish the ideal
milieu of the most fully developed legislative council was
recognized and rejected more than a decade before the
first council was created, in favor of a more prevalent
reality—the political leadership of the chief executive
and the continuing struggle and balancing of forces within internally leaderless legislatures.

The Nature of a Legislature

As for the legislatures themselves, the great diversity among the states makes generalization both difficult
and dangerous. The phase, "the legislature," does not
really mean exactly the same thing in New York that it
does in Kentucky or Kansas. Recognizing this, we can
generalize within limits. But in doing so we tend at
times to overlook the fact that a legislature is more
nearly a process (or a complex of processes) than a formal structure of organization, such as a bureaucracy.
Its inherent and essential nature may readily be obscured by too much attention to the voluminous facts so
easily mustered concerning its structure, membership,
and mechanics.

> A discussion of the work and defects of a state
> legislature carries one nowhere as long as the
> legislature is taken for what it purports to be

> —a body of men who deliberate upon and
> adopt law. . . .
>
> All phenomena of government are phenomena
> of groups pressing one another, forming one
> another, and pushing out new groups and
> group representatives . . . to mediate the
> adjustments. . . .
>
> There is not a law that is passed that is not
> the expression of force and force in tension.[9]

A legislature is an arena, and legislating is an endless
process of conflict and adjustment. In varying ways and
to varying degrees, the forces meet and merge within
the legislatures and outside them. Despite their great
appearances of similarity in form, procedure and product, the legislatures are, as processes, vastly diverse,
because the political forces at work within them and
about them vary much from state to state. The homogeneous politics of Kansas bears no striking resemblance
to the sometimes bitter brawling executive-legislative
battleground of Illinois.

In some states, where the cleavage among these
forces is relatively small and the interaction occurs substantially within the legislatures, legislative councils
are quite feasible. In Kansas as elsewhere, "Those concerned in government are still human beings. . . . They
have private interests to serve and interests of special
groups. . . ."[10] The Kansas council has not eliminated
the interplay of such interests. It has, however, helped
give it focus through hearings, orderly discussion, and
the elimination of the proverbial clutter which obscures
the session-time legislative process, and it has miti-
gated the extreme consequences of uninhibited legislative access by interests, through the provision of much
technical knowledge and some of the political knowledge
involved in legislating. It has helped eliminate crisis and

disorder through anticipation of issues, and it has added
continuity and perspective to the legislative process.

Yet these enviable contributions appear possible
only as a result of the relatively high degree of cohesive-
ness one finds in the political setting of the council and
legislature. Such states as Kansas are hardly typical.
Instead one often finds potent groups capable of and will-
ing to use steamroller tactics to obtain their legislative
aims; splintered bodies politic producing majorities for
decisions only by "trading and dealing;" underrepresen-
tation of some sectors of the population; great, persistent pressures to arrive at decisions if only to stop the
battle for the time, or to dispose of the overwhelming
volume of questions awaiting answers; and legislators
unbound by any "overarching party organization" who
are constituency-oriented, and often with a vengence.[11]
In such settings legislative decision-making is seldom
neat, simple, and dominated by rational concern with
technical facts.

Within the legislative arena there may be many
leaders, different kinds of leaders, and leaders acting
upon the legislature from outside it, seeking to shape
and influence decisions by the enactment of laws, or by
preventing the adoption of particular proposals.[12] The
decisions arrived at in the legislature are in themselves
composite results of the decisions made by individual
participants in the process. These, in turn, are based
upon available relevant knowledge of two kinds— "technical knowledge that defines the content of a policy issue;
and political knowledge of the relative strength of com-
peting claims and of the consequences of alternative decisions on a policy issue."[13] To the casual observer, the
results are sometimes baffling; "obviously technical"
questions may be decided on the basis of political knowledge which is far from evident. Patently simple specific
issues may be resolved upon the basis of murkily complex

political relations seemingly irrelevant to the content of
a particular policy. A man's vote on "right-to-work"
legislation may be determined by the prospect of getting
or losing a liquor license.

Technical premises furnished by legislative policy
staffs are thus never more than a portion of the basis
for decision-making — sometimes a major element and
at others of no real consequence. The legislative council process seeks the synthesis of technical and political knowledge. But in some places the synthesizing operation cannot be neatly structured, for reasons which
we have noted.

Yet technical knowledge is always one element of
the basis for decision-making, and its inexorably mounting significance over the years has been the fountain-
head of the efforts at legislative improvement covered
in this study. The legislature is an arena, but many of
the questions raised in it are essentially technical, and
while the high dramas are played in the center much
goes quietly on in the shadows. In making his case,
Bentley overstated it a bit. Many matters do not involve
the clash of interests on a significant scale. Of the
1100-odd pages of laws enacted by one recent assembly,
perhaps only five or six per cent reflect the outcome of
important struggles. Perhaps half involved some degree of review, negotiation, compromise. But page after
page of these statutes deals with mechanics, with housekeeping, with fundamentally non-controversial matters
of minor method and means. Some of these seemingly
innocuous items occasionally get drawn into the center
of the stage, inadvertently or otherwise, but only a few,
for there are far, far too many for it to be otherwise.
The problem of coping with these numerous matters is
largely one of a limited legislative span of control,
which can be extended greatly through technical staff
assistance, including research.

Hence, as the work of the Illinois Legislative Council indicates, a research staff which is not truly a council can be an eminently suitable alternative to one. Even where policy-proposing legislative councils are regarded as threats to other elements of leadership, legislatures and legislators must still have "the right to seek information useful in their deliberations, and to seek it independently if need be. . . ."[14] The impossibility of establishing a neatly structured system of cohesive legislative leadership does not obviate the need for technical knowledge, and for methods of screening out and expeditiously handling the bulk of non-controversial technical matters which come before the legislatures.

> Because I am so recently 'sprung' from a state legislature, people invariably ask me about the difference between service in the U.S. Senate and a typical state senate. If there is any one dividing characteristic, it is in the vastly superior information and assistance which are available to a United States Senator. State senators are on their own. United States Senators have the advantage of extensive and welltrained committee staffs, of the reference facilities of the Library of Congress, of the vigilant majority and minority conferences of their respective political parties.
>
> When I first entered the Senate, I was shocked to see bills gaveled to passage like pickets flashing past on a fence. 'Without objection, the bill is passed,' intoned the presiding officer with monotonous regularity. Then I began to realize that all such bills had been carefully screened prior to reaching the unanimous consent calendar. This was the result of elaborate staff work. It probably could not be risked in a state legislature, with so relatively few aides and researchers.[15]

The statement is a bit broad, but the assertation that state legislatures have a great need for information and staff assistance is true indeed.

In many states a combination of legislative research and other technical aid in such matters as bill-drafting makes sense, even though a legislative council does not.

> If the legislature wants a legislatively sponsored policy on a particular matter, a special study commission can be created. . . Governors whose staffs keep well informed on these developments are not likely to be caught off balance in policy planning. Governors have their own channels and means for influencing and courting these developments, including requesting the legislature to establish study commissions on matters of interest to governors.[16]

Interim committees have their limitations, and one test of an effective legislative council is their absence from the scene. It has been said that "more than 50% of interim committee assignments have been of little value,"[17] but in a recent year the various state legislatures appropriated a total of $2,307,232 for 177 interim committee studies,[18] and in a few cases such as Minnesota, legislative research organizations have come to function as secretariats for these bodies.

One further comment upon the informational needs of state legislatures and legislators is irresistable: The requirements and desires of the individual legislators for technical knowledge are quite easily overstated. The vision of the lost and lonely assembly-man hungering after knowledge as the hart panteth after water is a bit ingenuous, and as a foundation for legislative reform likely to be misleading. The typical legislator has neither need nor desire to be informed of all that pends or transpires within the assembly. Admittedly he "is not equipped to run down the technical details of the great volume of proposed legislation facing him at every session, nor to study carefully the broad governmental problems as they arise."[19] Nor is it necessary to assume the desirability, let alone the possibility, of thus equipping our amateur citizen legislator. Were this not true, our assemblies would have long ceased to operate. The individual legislator cares little about much or most of the legislative grist (particularly when he has ascertained its irrelevance to his own concerns), although he is likely to have an acute interest in some particular items of business, and to benefit from technical information concerning the se. True enough, somebody must study the problems broadly and keep in touch with myriad details, particularly in connection with efforts to exercise broad policy leadership or influence. But the assertion that a legislative council or research organization is to be valued because it enables the legislator to run down the technical details of a great volume of legislation or to study carefully all the broad problems "so that his final decisions can be based upon impartial information"[20] is a gentle fraud indeed.

The lack of any broad, persistent concern for technical premises on the part of untold numbers of legislators has probably contributed more than anything else to the atrophy of numerous legislative reference bureaus. We do not need means for making the individual legislator omniscient, but rather effective alternatives to the naive assumption of his unlimited wisdom and concern. Some of us still seek legislators patterned after Godwin's vision, or are at least unwilling to speak in terms of other assumptions. But legislative councils, legislative research agencies, and other sources of technical premises pertinent to legislative issues do not basically modify the individual legislator's span of attention and

concern so much as they make it more compatible with
the needs of the policy-making system. They do this in
several ways:

1. By studying the broad problems for him, on the
basis of continuing specialized efforts which the amateur
legislator is in no way able to provide, and which even
the professional legislator, as an individual, can only undertake in a limited way.

2. By running down the technical details not so
much "for him" but in lieu thereof, thereby helping win-
now the legislative grain in the course of bill-drafting,
research, and in the formulation of policy proposals.
Time and time again the legislative aides will indicate
in one way or another that "this is a technical matter,
of no political consequence," and so long as an appropriate aura of objectivity and neutrality is maintained,
and there are no gross mistakes, this usually suffices.[21]

3. Finally, staff sources of technical premises reduce
the legislator's—and the legislature's—dependence upon
interest groups with privileged access. By their presence and by their contributions they broaden the context within which individual policy questions may be considered and narrow the range of opportunity available
for grossly irresponsible or misrepresentative assertions and acts.

In short, councils and other agencies furnishing
part of the premises for legislative decision-making
help the legislatures cope with their acute span of control problem—a problem inseparably related to our
persistent dedication in most American states to the
ideal of the part-time citizen legislator. They do this
not primarily by modifying the intellectual competence
and ethical stature of the legislator, but by helping bring
these into balance with policy-making needs.

The Legislatures and the Making of Policy

> Policy . . . includes almost any matter for de-
> cision that requires the attention and consent
> of important actors on the scene, such as legis-
> lators, governors, or—when issues are de-
> termined by ballot—the voters. . . . Policy
> decisions commonly, although not exclusively,
> take the form of legislation adopted, so we are
> concerned here largely with the legislative
> process.[22]

The role of the state legislature in the making of
policy varies from place to place as well as from issue
to issue. It has certainly changed over time. In the
early days of American statehood the legislative initiation of policy proposals was a commonplace matter; today the delineation between proposal and disposal is
often sharp and clear; proposals emanate from many
sources, and the major role of the legislature is to
balance, compromise, and decide.

The extent to which policy proposals are initiated
by legislators varies greatly, although the popular
American assumption that the legislature is the prime
legitimate source of policy proposals appears to retain
wide acceptance. In some states there is substantial
concurrence of myth and reality, notably in connection
with the operation of legislative councils. In other cases
the governor and the administrative branch may be the
chief sources of policy proposals. Always, of course,
there are interests seeking to protect or extend their
concerns; and finally come the individual legislators
motivated to varying degrees by altruism, true belief,
or self-interest.

Legislative policy staffs appear to increase the exercise of legislative initiative in proposing policies, a
fact which probably has little inherent significance.

More important are the facts that such staffs, whether
councils or research organizations, (1) help anticipate
needs for policy action in a way that the legislature itself is seldom able to do, thereby contributing to the
avoidance of crises and ill-considered action, (2) help
furnish a perspective for the consideration of policy proposals, no matter where these originate, through the
marshalling of relatively objective data and knowledge
of the experience of other states, and (3) tend to become
"policy historians," through the accumulation of bill-
files and various other types of information of past proposals and their respective fates. The value of this last
service is best appreciated in its absence; it is one of
the real assets accruing from institutionalized legislative policy staffs. Finally, it is conceivable that to some
extent legislative policy staffs help protect the interests
of the underrepresented or unrepresented, by taking account of these in the course of research or program
planning. It is difficult to assess this assumption, but
it is also clear that legislative policy staffs cannot em-
bark upon militant crusades if they are to retain the
support of their clients.

Regardless of the source of policy proposals,

> lawmaking is central to policy making. Not
> that there are not other ways of making
> policy. . . .

> Nonetheless, under the principles of repre-
> sentative government, it is the state legisla-
> ture that is expected to settle most policy
> questions.[23]

The state legislatures are "the courts for deciding
what ought to be done."[24]

Most commonly these institutions and their processes work themselves out to the conclusion
that, in large part, what is ought to continue to
be. However, the processes regularly produce
moderate and small changes in the expected actions of the state government, and there are always possibilities of major changes in policy.[25]

In our system, there is simply no adequate substitute
for the state legislature, although there is great latitude
for variation in the role of the legislature in policy—making. No matter how domineering the governor, or how
blatant the interests, the legislature remains a significant force. In the legislative arena the exercise of political power is at least to some degree ordered and re-
gularized. The legislature and the process of selecting
its members always afford some opportunity for mobilizing public demands and desires. The most powerful interests are forced to run the legislative gantlet, or to
clash perhaps within the arena. Policy acts and actors
must always stand exposed—or in jeopardy of exposure
—to the public gaze in the course of legislative proceed-
ings. In all the legislatures there is some amelioration
of extremes and blending of interests. In the last analysis the policy-making significance of the legislatures
does not lie in their role in initiating proposals, but
rather in the furnishing of a means for reviewing and
ratifying, for forcing balance and compromise, and for
constraining and restraining extremist forces.

The legislative process is a means for making almost infinite numbers of inescapable decisions, for the
absence of a positive decision about a pending issue is
in itself for the time decisive. The quality of the decisions is obviously related to the quality of the process.

In the past half-century, and particularly in the last
25 years, the most significant substantive improvements

in the legislative processes of our American states have
been the development of technical services and policy
staff aids, and their reinforcement by such arrangements as the Council of State Governments. In some
places the length of legislative sessions has been extended, and the amount of secretarial and related assistance available to legislators has been increased.
Some reapportionment has occurred. But there has been
only one case of radical legislative reorganization, and
after more than twenty years this unicameral experiment shows no signs of spreading. Finally, the problem of an inadequate political focus at the state level of
government noted by Bryce is certainly no less acute today in many states than it was half a century ago.

      Yet it is only fair and accurate to admit that policy
staff devices can never solve some basic problems of
the various state legislative institutions, such as gross
malapportionment, inordinate limitations on legislative
power and responsibility, and naïve assumptions about
legislative compensation and the inherent, unqualified
virtue of the amateur legislator functioning with the
most limited assistance at infrequent intervals.

      As for the future:

> Institutional reconstruction [of state legisla-
> tures] may have over the long pull significant
> secondary influences on informal systems of
> political leadership. Insofar as tinkering with
> the formal apparatus of government can have
> such derivative consequences, the odds are
> that the legislature is the point with the great-
> est potential leverage.[26]

One conceivable consequence of basic legislative reorganization might be a strengthening and rationalizing
of the party system which, by its inadequacy and unrepresentativeness in many states, seems to preclude the

political focusing which is so important to responsible, dynamic government.

After all is said and done, the fundamental problems of our state governments are political problems.

> The men we elect to office and the circumstances we create that affect their work determine the nature of popular government. Let there be emphasis upon those we elect to office. Legislators, governors, and other such elective functionaries ultimately fix the basic tone and character of state government.[27]

Staff policy aids alter very little the basic tone and character of state government.

The States and the Governmental System

The legislatures remain essential elements of our rather diverse states and the states continue to be vital parties to our ever changing system of government. No radical reformation of the basic system seems in sight.

Yet the literature on American state government continues to be tinged with titles such as these: "The Decay of State Governments,"[28] and The Crisis of the States.[29] Some of us are vexed, when we think of it, by the question, "Are We Maintaining Our Federal System?"[30] In the last years of his life, Professor Leonard D. White warned insistently that "if present trends continue for another quarter century, the states may be left hollow shells,. . . dependent upon the federal treasury for their support."[31] He asserted that

> the states have lost status, prestige, and power in the federal system, and are today weaker members of the federal partnership than they

were a half-century ago. They have lost so much, indeed, that most competent observers at home and abroad have declared that American federalism is approaching its end, that we are destined to be governed by Washington, and that the states will survive primarily as field agents of the national government.[32]

Some critics have gone even further, if this be possible. As early as 1940 Harold Laski observed that "federalism is obsolete." In 1949 a very able Washington correspondent, Roscoe Drummond, concluded that ". . .our federal system no longer exists and has no more chance of being brought back into existence than an apple pie can be put back on the apple tree." [33]

The fact that the system and the place of the states in it has been changing is in itself hardly cause for surprise or alarm. It always has been undergoing adaptation, and there is surely as much cause for concern in the loss of suppleness in the framework of our governmental system, should this occur, as in the fact of change.

As for the centralizing trend of the 20th Century, it was predicted by Woodrow Wilson as long ago as 1884, as the inevitable response to already pressing problems, including the need for ". . . the regulation of our vast system of commerce and manufacture, the control of giant corporations, the restraining of monopoly . . . , and many other like national concerns."[34] "It seems probable to many that, whether by constitutional amendment, or by still further flights of construction, yet broader territory will at no very distant day be assigned to the federal government."[35]

Those who have raised a hue and cry against the downfall of our system have seldom sought to distinquish between changes produced by inexorable environmental forces and those resulting from the reiterated inadequacies of our state governments. The U.S. Department of Agriculture, our multifold national resource development programs, the Interstate Commerce Commission, social security, the FBI, the Bureau of Public Roads — such things are not the results of a fall from virtue by the states, nor would any conceivable amount of state governmental reform have eliminated the likelihood of their development. Some of the persistently voiced concerns over the capacity of our states to govern are sentimental expressions of regret for the decline of a past viewed as glorious. More are products of earnest conservatism (and sometimes rabid reactionaryism) striving to use plausible means for restricting national centralization of American government.

Centralization has its admitted disadvantages and dangers, and much good has come from efforts to resist it — including the Council of State Governments, for example, and a whole series of earnest efforts to improve the quality of state government. The record of the Kestnbaum Commission of a few years ago under scored both the non-rational fervor of some of the proponents of states' rights and the unlikelihood of any radical decentralization of contemporary domestic functions of the American national government. In its rather judicious and hence undramatic report, this Commission on Intergovernmental Relations repeatedly admitted the nature and consequences of the national interest, at the same time observing that even where this requires national action, "the initiative, energy, and competence of State and local governments may help to determine whether the National role is to be minor or major, cooperative or dominant."[36]

To the extent that concern over the consequences of national centralization produces pressure for reform among the states it is of course good. But "The strengthening of States and local governments is essentially a

task for the States themselves,"[37] and diversity among
the states in politics, resources, and governmental competence will continue to produce centralizing pressures,
as well as responses. After all,

> The American people are not boiling with con-
> cern about the workings of their state govern-
> ments. In competition for public interest and
> attention the governments of the American
> states come off a poor second-best against
> the performance of the finished professionals
> who operate in Washington.[38]

Yet the states show no signs of foundering. Some
of them have lurched along for nearly 200 years, sur-
viving crisis after crisis, and disasters beyond recall.
The vast emergency of the 1930's which produced such
heady proposals as William Yandell Elliott's Need for
Constitutional Reform[39] -also added a great deal of vitality to the states themselves. This has come in part
from various forms of federal aid and federal reinforcement of state and local administrative mechanisms. But
even more, the very burgeoning of governmental duties
and concerns in the 20th Century, and especially in the
past 25 years, has expanded the role of the states. Their
tasks in lawmaking and law enforcement, in education,
highways, welfare, mental health, and a hundred fields
of regulation have not shrunk. Whatever the plight of
the states, they are not withering away; and whatever
our opinions about their adequacy and competence, the
final test of a government must always be survival.

By all the indices the functions of state government
have grown tremendously, and the trend continues. In
1915 the states were spending $ 11.31 per capita (in
terms of 1947-49 dollar value). By 1941 the amount had
increased to $ 42.90—and it doubled again between 1941
and 1954.[40]

One aspect of this growth has been the emergence
of the states as "financial middlemen." American local
governments currently obtain from state sources about
25 per cent of their revenues. The states themselves
are dependent upon the national government for about
12 1/2 per cent of their own receipts.[41]

The scope of state administrative activity has
been growing substantially. The states employ a mil-
lion workers in the aggregate; and both state expenditures and state employment have been expanding in
the post-World War II era at rates faster than those of
either national or local government.[42]

The American states today are not threatened by
the erosive consequences of national centralization—
the real challenge they face is growth and its effects.
A constantly expanding scope of activity produces increased needs for wise policy and effective administration. It adds greatly to the problems of coordination. It
increases the demand for resources and the difficulty of
allocating them effectively. Population growth produces
needs for added governmental activity at the same time
that the existing citizenry demands an increased and
quality of services. Continuing specialization and diver-
sification in society make the structuring of the political
process more difficult than before. These are some of
the dimensions of the true problem facing the American
states.

In the last analysis this problem is political, and its
various relative solutions must be largely found within
our diverse states and their national setting. Legislative councils will play their part, although it is not
likely to be greatly enlarged, and the use of other legislative policy staffs is bound to grow in the years ahead.
Yet these devices will remain essentially only one
means for attacking exquisitely complex problems. They
are indeed valuable, and with them we may manage to

help prop up our legislative edifices for years to come, but councils and other policy staffs are not the elixir in which the basic problems of our fair states will be dissolved.

Notes

1. Key, op. cit., p. 12.

2. Frederick H. Guild, "Legislative Councils; Objectives and Accomplishments," State Government (September, 1949), pp. 219-226.

3. For example, the Wisconsin Legislative Reference Library is part of the state's Free Library Commission. For other examples see: "Table 1. Permanent Legislative Service Agencies," Book of the States 1958-1959, pp. 61-69.

4. In Illinois three or four research memoranda are prepared for individual legislators for every major report submitted to the full assembly.

5. David B. Truman, The Governmental Process (New York: Knopf), p. 325.

6. Karl A. Bosworth, "Law Making in State Governments," The Forty-eight States: Their Tasks as Policy Makers and Administrators, Report of the American Assembly (New York: Columbia University, 1955), p. 103.

7. Interview, Ames, Iowa, August 23, 1954.

8. "Iowa Legislative Service Agency," State Government, XXCIII (June, 1955), p. 144.

9. Arthur L. Bentley, The Process of Government (Chicago: University of Chicago Press, 1908; reissued, Bloomington, Indiana: Principia Press, 1949), pp. 163, 300, 202. See also Bertram M. Gross, The Legislative Struggle (New York: McGraw-Hill, 1953), esp. pp. ix, 5-9, and Truman, op. cit., pp. 188-193.

10. John Dewey, The Public and its Problems (New York: Henry Holt, 1927, p. 76.

11. Karl A. Bosworth's discerning essay, "Law Making in State Governments," op. cit., discusses these common characteristics of state legislatures; see p. 86. Regarding the typically localistic orientation of legislators, see Truman, op. cit., p. 325.

12. See Truman, "The Dynamics of Access in the Legislative Process," op. cit., Ch. 11, pp. 321-351.

13. Ibid., p. 334.

14. Bosworth, op. cit., p. 103.

15. Richard L. Neuberger, "Twentieth Century Legislatures for Twentieth Century Problems," Streamlining State Legislatures, Report of a Conference (Berkeley: University of California, 1956), p. 68.

16. Ibid.

17. Zeller, op. cit., p. 139.

18. State Government (April, 1955), p. 96.

19. Streamlining State Legislatures, op. cit., p. 108.

20. Ibid.

21. As Norman Meller points out, "In point of fact, their own value judgments unobtrusively but consistently enter into the formulation of the product of the legislative bodies they assist," although they "generally continue to profess scientific detachment from values." "The Policy Position of Legislative Service Agenices," Western Political Quarterly, V (March, 1952), 109, 111. He proceeds to observe that "Repeated questioning of the agency's good faith will undermine its further usefulness," (p. 116) which is certainly true, and much more significant than the maintenance of true objectivity, which is impossible anyhow. It is the aura that counts—along with freedom from blunders.

22. Bosworth, op. cit., p. 85.

23. James W. Fesler, "The Challenge to the States," The Forty-eight States, op. cit., p. 9. Italics added.

24. Bosworth, op. cit., p. 85.

25. Ibid.

26. Key, op. cit., p. 283. See pp. 283-286 for a
more detailed discussion of possible consequences of
legislative restructuring.

27. Ibid., p. 10.

28. Richard L. Neuberger, "The Decay of State
Governments," Harpers, (October, 1953), pp. 34-41.

29. Leonard D. White, The Crisis of the States
(Lexington: Bureau of Government Research, 1954).

30. "Are We Maintaining our Federal System?"
State Government, XXII (January, 1949), 1. Special Supplement.

31. Leonard D. White, The States and the Nation,
Edward Douglas White Lectures (Baton Rouge: Louisiana State University Press, 1953), p. 3.

32. White, The Crisis of the States, op. cit., p. 1.

33. Quoted in "Are We Maintaining Our Federal
System?," op. cit., p. 1.

34. Woodrow Wilson, Congressional Government
(15th ed., Boston: Houghton Mifflin Co., 1900), p. 55.

35. Ibid., p. 154-155.

36. A Report to the President for Transmittal to
the Congress, The Commission on Intergovernmental
Relations (Washington: Government Printing Office,
June, 1955), p. 36.

37. Ibid., p. 37.

38. Key, op. cit., p. 1.

39. Elliott, The Need for Constitutional Reform,
op. cit., a proposal for the reorganization of the states
along regional lines which was quite impractical at the
same time that it set forth discerning observations
about the regional character of American politics.

40. "The Task of the State Legislature," Streamlining State Legislatures, op. cit., p. 9. See also Solomon Fabricant, The Trend of Government Activity in
the United States Since 1900, op. cit.

41. Key, <u>op</u>. <u>cit</u>., p. 8.

42. York Willbern, "Administration in State Government," <u>The</u> <u>Forty-eight</u> <u>States</u>, op. cit., p. 111.

BIBLIOGRAPHY

Books

Alden, Edmund K. The World's Representative Assemblies of Today: A Study in Comparative Legislation. Baltimore: John Hopkins Press, 1893.

Allen, Robert S. Our Sovereign States. New York: Vanguard Press, 1949.

Andrews, Charles M. The Colonial Period in American History. 4 vols. New Haven: Yale University Press, 1934-38.

Baldwin, Simeon E. Modern Political Institutions. Boston: Little, Brown and Co., 1898.

Bentley, Arthur L. The Process of Government. Bloomington, Indiana: University of Chicago Press, 1908, reissued, Principia Press, 1949.

The Book of the States, 1935, 1940-41, 1948-49, 1950-51, 1952-53, 1954-55, 1956-57, 1958-59. Chicago: The Council of State Governments.

Bromage, Arthur W. State Government and Administration in the U.S. New York: Harper Brothers, 1936.

Brownlow, Louis, A Passion For Anonymity. Chicago: University of Chicago Press, 1958.

Bryce, James. The American Commonwealth. Vol. I. New York: MacMillan and Co., 1891.

Buck, A. E. The Reorganization of State Governments in the United States. New York: Columbia University Press, 1938.

Chamberlain, Joseph P. Legislative Processes, National and State. New York: D. Appleton-Century Co., 1936.

Childs, Richard S. Civic Victories. New York: Harper Brothers, 1952.

Clark, Jane Perry. The Rise of a New Federalism. New York: Columbia University Press, 1938.

Commager, Henry Steele. The American Mind. New
    Haven: Yale University Press. 1950.

Commons, John R. Myself. New York: The MacMillan
    Co., 1934.

Croly, Herbert D. Progressive Democracy. New York:
    The MacMillan Co., 1914.

Dealey, James Q. Growth of American State Constitu-
    tions. Boston: Ginn and Co., 1915.

DeGrazia, Alfred. Public and Republic. New York:
    Alfred A. Knopf, 1951.

deTocqueville, Alexis. Democracy in America. 2 vols.
    Edited by Phillips Bradley. New York: Alfred
    A. Knopf, 1945.

Dewey, John. The Public and Its Problems. New York:
    Henry Holt, 1927.

Dickerson, Oliver M. American Colonial Government
    1696-1765. Cleveland: A. H. Clark Co., 1912.

Dodd, Walter F. State Government. New York: The
    Century Company, 1928.

Elliott, William Yandell. The Need for Constitutional
    Reform. New York: Whittlesey House, 1935.

Fabricant, Solomon. The Trend of Government Activity
    in the United States Since 1900. New York: Na-
    tional Bureau of Economic Research, 1952.

Farmer, Hallie. The Legislative Process in Alabama.
    University, Alabama: Bureau of Public Admin-
    istration, University of Alabama, 1949.

Ford, Henry J. Representative Government. New York:
    Henry Holt, 1924.

Frankfurter, Felix. The Public and Its Government.
    New Haven: Yale University Press, 1930.

Freund, Ernst. Standards of American Legislation.
    Chicago: University of Chicago Press, 1917.

Friedrich, Carl J. Constitutional Government and De-
    mocracy. Boston: Little, Brown and Co., 1941.

Galloway, George. Congress at the Crossroads. New
    York: Thos. Y. Crowell, 1946.

_____. The Legislative Process in Congress. New
    York: Thos. Y. Crowell, 1953.

Gettell, Raymond G. History of American Political
    Thought. New York: The Century Company,
    1928.

Graves, W. Brooke. American State Government. 4th
    ed. Boston: D.C. Heath and Co., 1953.

_____. Uniform State Action. Chapel Hill: University
    of North Carolina Press, 1934.

Gross, Bertam M. The Legislative Struggle. New York:
    McGraw-Hill Publishing Co., 1953.

Harlow, Ralph V. The History of Legislative Methods
    in the Period Before 1825. New Haven: Yale
    University Press, 1917.

Hinderaker, Ivan. Party Politics. New York: Henry
    Holt, 1956.

Holcombe, A. N. State Government in the U.S. 3rd ed.
    New York: The MacMillan Co., 1935.

Ilbert, Sir Courtenay. Legislative Methods and Forms.
    London: Oxford University Press, 1901.

Kaiser, J. B. Law, Legislative Reference, and Munici-
    pal Reference Libraries. Boston: Boston Book
    Co., 1914.

Key, V. O. American State Politics: An Introduction.
    New York: Alfred A. Knopf, 1956.

Leek, J. H. Legislative Reference Work, A Compara-
    tive Study. Philadelphia: University of Penn-
    sylvania, 1925.

Lipson, Leslie. The American Governor From Figure-
    head to Leader. Chicago: University of Chicago
    Press, 1939.

Loewenstein, Karl. The Balance Between Legislative
    and Executive Power. Chicago: University of
    Chicago Press, 1938.

Luce, Robert. Legislative Principles, The History and
    Theory of Lawnmaking. Boston: Houghton
    Mifflin, 1930.

_____. Legislative Procedure. Boston: Houghton
    Mifflin, 1922.

_____. Legislative Problems: Development, Status
    and Trend of ... Lawnmaking Powers. Boston,
    Houghton Mifflin, 1935.

McCarthy, Charles. The Wisconsin Idea. New York:
    The MacMillan Co., 1912.

McLaughlin, Andrew C. The Foundations of American
    Constitutionalism. New York: New York Uni-
    versity Press, 1932.

Merriam, Charles F. A History of American Political
    Theories. New York: The MacMillan Co., 1915.

Mill, John Stuart. Considerations on Representative
    Government. London: Longmans, Green and
    Co., 1872.

Moran, Thomas F. The Rise and Development of the
    Bicameral System in America. Baltimore:
    Johns Hopkins University Press, 1895.

Nevins, Allen. The American States During and After
    the Revolution 1775-1789. New York: The Mac-
    Millan Co., 1924.

Osgood, Herbert L. The American Colonies in the Sev-
    enteenth Century. 3 vols. New York: The Mac-
    Millan Co., 1904-1907.

_____. The American Colonies in the Eighteenth
    Century. 2 vols. New York: Columbia Univer-
    sity Press, 1924.

Parrington, Vernon L. Main Currents in American
    Thought. New York: Harcourt, Brace and Co.,
    1927.

Patterson, Caleb Perry. The Constitutional Principles
    of Thomas Jefferson. Austin: University of
    Texas Press, 1953.

Peel, Roy V. State Government Today. Albuquerque:
    University of New Mexico Press, 1948.

Ransone, Coleman B. Jr. The Office of Governor in the
    South. University, Alabama: Bureau of Public
    Administration, University of Alabama, 1951.

Reed, Thomas H. (ed.). Legislatures and Legislative
    Problems. Chicago: University of Chicago
    Press, 1933.

Reinsch, Paul S. American Legislatures and Legisla-
    tive Methods. New York: The Century Company,
    1907.

Rossiter, Clinton. The First American Revolution.
    Part I, Seedtime of the Republic. New York:
    Harcourt, Brace, and Co., 1953.

Senning, John P. The One-House Legislature. New
    York: McGraw-Hill Publishing Co., 1937.

Smith, T. V. The Legislative Way of Life. Chicago:
    University of Chicago Press, 1940.

Stephens, C. Ellis. Sources of the Constitution of the
    United States. New York: The MacMillan Co.,
    1894.

Stewart, Frank M. A Half Century of Municipal Re-
    form. Berkeley: University of California Press,
    1950.

Thorpe, Francis Newton. Constitutional History of the
    United States. Vol. I. Chicago: Callaghan and
    Co., 1901.

_____. The Federal and State Constitutions, Colonial
    Charters, and Other Organic Laws. Washington:
    Government Printing Office, 1909.

Truman, David B. The Governmental Process, New
    York, Knopf, 1951.

Turner, Frederick Jackson. The Frontier in American
    History. New York: Henry Holt and Co., 1920.

Waldo, Dwight. The Administrative State. New York:
    Ronald Press, 1948.

Walker, Harvey. The Legislative Process, Lawmaking
    in the U.S. New York: Ronald Press, 1948.

Weber, Gustavius A. Organized Efforts for the Improve-
    ment of Methods of Administration in the U.S.
    New York: D. Appleton & Co., 1919.

White, Leonard D. The States and the Nation, Baton
    Rouge, Louisiana State University Press, 1953.

Willoughby, W. F. Principles of Legislative Organiza-
    tion and Administration. Washington: The
    Brookings Institution, 1934.

Wilson, Woodrow. Congressional Government. 15th ed.
    Boston: Houghton Mifflin, 1913.

Winslow, Clinton I. State Legislature Committees, A
    Study in Procedure. Baltimore: Johns Hopkins
    University Press, 1931.

Wight, Martin. Development of the Legislative Council,
    1606-1945. London: Faber and Faber, 1946.

Zeller, Belle (ed.). American State Legislatures. Re-
    port of the Committee on American Legislatures,
    American Political Science Association. New
    York: Thomas Y. Crowell Co., 1954.

                    Bibliographies

Darity, Ione E. State Organization and Administration.
    A list of references on selected problems. Ann
    Arbor: University of Michigan Bureau of Gov-
    ernment Service, 1950.

Graves, Wm. Brooke, Small, Norman J., and Dowell, E.
    Foster. American State Government and Admin-
    istration. A state by state bibliography. Chicago:
    Council of State Governments, 1949.

Guild, F. H. Legislative Councils: An Article and a Bib-
    liography. Topeka: Kansas Legislative Council, 1944.

Weiner, Grace. Administration Reorganization of State
    Governments: A Bibliography. Chicago: Coun-
    cil of State Governments, 1948.

                Selected Public Documents

American Bar Association Bill Drafting and Legislative
    Bureaus. Report of the Special Committee on
    Legislative Drafting of the American Bar Associa-
    tion, 1913, S. Doc. 262. 63rd Cong., 2nd Sess.
    Washington: Government Printing Office.

Bureau of Legislative Information (ed.). Yearbook of
the State of Indiana, 1917. Indianapolis: Wm. B.
Burford, 1918.

The Commission on Intergovernmental Relations. A Report to the President for Transmittal to the Congress. Washington: Government Printing Office,
1955.

Corrick, Franklin. Forms, Rules and Committee Assignments of the 1953-54 Kansas Legislative
Council. Topeka, Kansas, June, 1953.

Guild, Frederick H. The Development of the Legislative Council Idea. Research Department, Kansas Legislative Council. Topeka, Kansas, 1938.

Kansas Legislative Council. Kansas' Experiment With
a Legislative Council. Bulletin No. 42 of the Research Department. Topeka, Kansas, August,
1936.

Kentucky Legislative Research Commission. The Story
of Kentucky's Constitution. Frankfort, Kentucky,
1952.

Minnesota Efficiency in Government Commission. Recommendations: How to Achieve Greater Efficiency and Economy in Minnesota's Government.
St. Paul, Minnesota, December, 1950.

National Resources Committee. Research— A National
Resource. Washington: Government Printing Office, 1938.

_____. State Planning and Accomplishments. Wash-
ington: Government Printing Office, 1936.

National Resources Planning Board. State Planning: A
Review of Activities and Progress. Washington:
Government Printing Office, 1935.

Thornton, Herschel V. Legislative Organization and Procedure. Report of Constitutional Survey Committee. Oklahoma City: State Legislative Council,
1940.

U.S. Congress, House, Committee on the Library. Congressional Reference Bureau Hearings ... on

Various Bills Proposing Establishment of a Con-
    gress Reference Bureau. 62d Cong., 1st Sess.
    Washington: Government Printing Office, 1912.

U.S. Congress, Senate. Report and Hearings on a Legis-
    lative Reference Bureau. Senate Report 1271.
    62d Cong., 3d Sess. Washington: Government
    Printing Office, 1913.

U.S. Congress, Senate, Committee on the Library.
    Legislative Drafting Bureau and Legislative
    Reference Division of Library of Congress.
    Hearings on S. 8337 and S. 8335. 62d Cong., 2d
    Sess. Washington: Government Printing Office,
    1913.

Reports

Atwood, Albert W. and Joseph McGoldrick. What is the
    Matter with the State Legislatures? Government
    Series III, Lecture No. 10 Chicago: The Uni-
    versity of Chicago Press, 1933.

Buck, A. E. Administrative Consolidation in State Gov-
    ernments. Technical Pamphlet Series No. 2.
    New York: National Municipal League, 1938.

_____. Modernizing Our State Legislatures. Pamphlet
    Series No. 4. Philadelphia: American Academy
    of Political and Social Science, 1936.

Carroll, Daniel B. The Unicameral Legislature of Ver-
    mont. Proceedings Historical Society, New
    Series Vol. III. Mt. Pelier, Vt.: History Society,
    1933.

Culver, Margaret S. Proposals for Legislative Reorgani-
    zation. Survey. Chicago: Council of State Gov-
    ernments, 1939.

Davey, Harold W. Helping Iowa's Legislature. Iowa
    Economic Studies. Iowa City: Advisory Council
    for Iowa Economic Studies, 1949.

Edwards, William H. The State Reorganization Move-
    ment. Bismarck: University of North Dakota,
    1928.

The Forty-eight States: Their Tasks as Policy Makers
     and Administrators. Report of the American As-
     sembly, Columbia University. New York: Co-
     lumbia University, 1955.

Gove, Samuel K., and Steiner, Gilbert Y. The Illinois
     Legislative Process. Urbana: Institute of Gov-
     ernment, The University of Illinois, 1954.

Guild, Frederick H. Legislative Procedure in Kansas.
     Lawrence: Bureau of Government Research,
     University of Kansas, 1946.

Haines, Charles G. The Movement for the Reorganiza-
     tion of State Administration. Bulletin of the Uni-
     versity of Texas, Government Research Series
     No. 17. Austin: The University of Texas, 1920.

Horack, Frank E. Reorganization of State Government
     in Iowa. Iowa City: State Historical Society of
     Iowa, 1914.

Larsen, Christian L., and Ryan, Miles F. Aids for State
     Legislators. Columbia: Bureau of Public Ad-
     ministration, University of South Carolina, 1947.

Laurent, Eleanore V. Legislative Reference Work in the
     United States. Chicago: The Council of State
     Governments, 1939.

Legislative Structure and Procedure of Michigan. The
     Michigan Legislature. Lansing: Michigan State
     Bar Association, 1940.

Lewis, Henry W. Legislative Committees in North
     Carolina. Chapel Hill: University of North Caro-
     lina, 1952.

McHenry, Dean E. The Legislative Council Idea. Berke-
     ley: The University of California, 1934.

Model State Constitution. 4th ed. New York: National
     Municipal League, 1945.

O'Rourke, Lawrence W. Legislative Assistance, Some
     Staff Services Provided for Legislatures. Los
     Angeles: Bureau of Government Research, Uni-
     versity of California, 1951.

Our State Legislatures. Report of Committee on

Legislative Processes and Procedures. Chicago: The Council of State Governments, 1946.
Also revised edition, 1948.

The Problem of Legislative Reference and Bill-Drafting
Service. A Report of a Committee of the American Bar Association, 1913.

A Progress Report on State Reorganization in 1950. Chicago: Council of State Governments, 1950.

The Reorganization of Congress. A Report of the Committee on Congress of the American Political
Science Association. Washington: Public Affairs Press, 1945.

Reorganizing State Government. Chicago: Council of
State Governments, 1950.

Revised Preliminary Report, Special Committee on Or-
ganization of Legislative Services. Legislative
Service Conference. Chicago: Council of State
Governments, 1953.

Richards, Allen R. Legislative Services with Special
Emphasis on the Problems of New Mexico. Albuquerque: University of New Mexico, 1953.

Sterne, Simon. Our Methods of Legislation and Their
Defects. New York: New York Municipal Society, 1874.

Streamlining State Legislatures. Report of a Conference
Held at the University of California, Berkeley,
October 27-29, 1955. Berkeley: University of
California, 1956.

Weeks, Oliver Douglas. Research in the American State
Legislature Process. Ann Arbor: J. W. Edwards,
1947.

Articles

Adams, James Truslow. "A Way Out," American Le-
tion Magazine, XXIV (March, 1938), 8-9, 37, 39.

_____. "A Third Choice," State Government, XI (Janu-
ary, 1938), 3-4.

Allen, Henry J. "Modernizing the State Legislature," The Rotarian, LIV (January, 1939), 22-23.

Bates, Frank G. "Legislative Organization and Procedure," American Political Science Review, X (February, 1916), 120-123.

Brown, L. F. "Ideas of Representation from Elizabeth to Charles II," Journal of Modern History, XI (1939), 23-40.

Bruncken, Ernest. "Defective Methods of Legislation," American Political Science Review, III (1909), 167.

_____. "Some Neglected Factors in Law-Making," American Political Science Review, VIII (May, 1914), 222-237.

Cleland, Ethel. "Bill Drafting," American Political Science Review, VIII (May, 1914), 244-251.

_____. "Legislative Reference"(survey), American Political Science Review, VII (August, 1913), 444-447, and X (February, 1916), 110-113.

"Connecticut Adopts Legislative Council," National Municipal Review, XXVI (May, 1937), 253.

Davey, Harold W. "The Legislative Council Movement in the United States, 1933-1953," American Political Science Review, XLVII (September, 1953), 785-797.

Dodds, Harold W. "Procedure in State Legislatures," Supplement #1, Annals, American Academy of Political and Social Science, May, 1918, pp. 1-112.

Dorr, Harold M. "A Legislative Council for Michigan," American Political Science Review, XXVIII (April, 1934), 270-275.

Fairlie, James A. "Legislative and Municipal Reference Agencies," American Political Science Review, XVII (May, 1923), 303-308.

_____. "The State Governor," Michigan Law Review, X (March and April, 1912), 370-383; 458-475.

Fisher, E. A. "Legislative Reference in the United

States," American Political Science Review, III
(March, 1909), 223.

Freund, Ernst. "Principles of Legislation," American
    Political Science Review, X (February, 1916),
    1-19.

_____. "The Problem of Intelligent Legislation," Ameri-
    can Political Science Review, IX (January, 1915),
    69.

Gallagher, Hubert. "Legislative Councils," National Mu-
    nicipal Review, XXIV (March, 1935), 147-151.

Gaus, John M. "The Wisconsin Executive Council,"
    American Political Science Review, XXVI (Octo-
    ber, 1932), 914-920.

Glaser, Ferdinand H. "Our Annual Meeting at Indiana-
    polis," National Municipal Review, X (January,
    1921), 9-21.

_____. "Our Moot State Constitutional Convention,"
    National Municipal Review, IX (February, 1920),
    66-68.

Graves, W. Brooke. "Our State Legislators," Annals,
    American Academy of Political and Social Science,
    CVC (January, 1938), i-xi.

Guild, Frederick H. "The Development of the Legislative
    Council Idea," Annals, American Academy of Po-
    litical and Social Science, CVC (January, 1938),
    144-150.

_____. "Legislative Councils," State Government, IX
    (June, 1936), 132.

_____. "Legislative Councils: Objectives and Accom-
    plishments," State Government, September, 1949,
    pp. 217-219, 226.

Haynes, G. H. "Representation in State Legislatures,"
    Annals, American Academy of Political and So-
    cial Science, XV (1900), 204-235.

"Iowa Legislative Service Agency," State Government,
    XXCIII (June, 1955), 144.

Jameson, J. Franklin. "Origin of the Standing Committees

System in American Legislative Bodies," Political Science Quarterly, IX (June, 1894), 245-267.

Kammerer, Gladys M. "The Development of a Legislative Research Arm," Journal of Politics, XII (Autumn, 1950), 652-667.

_____. "Kentucky's Legislature Under the Spotlight," Kentucky Law Journal, XXXIX (November, 1950), 45-63.

_____. "Legislative Oversight of Administration in Kentucky," Public Administration Review, X (Summer, 1950), 169-175.

_____. "Right About Face in Kentucky," National Municipal Review, XXXVII (June, 1948), 303-308.

Kelly, Alice. "Flash Voting," State Government, III (October, 1930), 7-8.

Kneier, Charles M. "Illinois Legislation Council Completes Its First Year," National Municipal Review, XXVIII (September, 1939), 640-645.

Lapp, John A. "Making Legislators Law Makers," Annals, American Academy of Political and Social Science, LXIV (March, 1916), 172-183.

Lee, Frederic Paddock. "The Office of the Legislative Council," Columbia Law Review, XXIX (1929), 381-403.

Leek, J. H. "The Legislative Reference Bureau in Recent Years," American Political Science Review, XX (November, 1926), 823-831.

"Legislative Councils for Virginia and Kentucky," National Municipal Review, XXV (July, 1936), 425.

"The Legislative Councils in Action," State Government, XVI (February, 1943), 34, 45-48.

Meller, Norman. "The Policy Position of Legislative Service Agencies," Western Political Quarterly, V (March, 1952), 109-123.

Neuberger, Richard L. "The Decay of State Governments," Harpers, October, 1953, pp. 34-41.

"Proposals for Model State Constitution. Progress Report

of Committee on State Government," National Municipal Review, IX (November, 1920), 711-715.

"Research Appropriations," State Government, XXVII (April, 1955), 96.

Rodgers, Jack W. "Assistance for the State Legislature," American Bar Association Journal, XLII (November, 1956), 1086-1088.

Rowell, Chester H. "Responsible Legislative Leadership," State Government, VII (June, 1934), editorial.

Shull, Charles W. "Legislative Council in Michigan," National Municipal Review, XXII (November, 1933), 570-571.

Smith, David W. "The Constitutionality of Legislative Councils," Western Political Quarterly, VIII (March, 1955), 68-81.

Sorauf, Frank J. "Extra-Legal Political Parties in Wisconsin," American Political Science Review, XLVIII (September, 1954), 692-704.

Spicer, George W. "Gubernatorial Leadership in Virginia," Public Administration Review, I (Autumn, 1941), 441-457.

Stafford, Paul T. "Modern Reconstruction of State Government," Annals, American Academy of Political and Social Science, CVC (January, 1938), 198-204.

Toepel, M. G. "The Legislative Reference Library: Serving Wisconsin," Wisconsin Law Review, January, 1951, pp. 114-124.

Toll, Henry W. "Today's Legislatures," Annals, American Academy of Political and Social Science, CVC (January, 1938), 1-10.

Tucker, Ray. "The Men Who Make Our Laws," Annals, American Academy of Political and Social Science, CLXIX (September, 1933), 47-54.

Walker, Harvey. "Kansas Shows The Way," Business Week, December 4, 1937, p. 37.

_____. "Legislative Councils—An Appraisal," National Municipal Review, XXVIII (December, 1939), 839-842.

_____. "Modernizing the State Legislature," The Rotarian, LIV (January, 1939), 22-23.

Weeks, O. Douglas. "Recent Developments in the State Legislative Process," State Government, XVI (July, 1943), 162-166.

White, Howard. "Relations Between the Governor and the Legislature in the Model Constitution," National Municipal Review, XV (August, 1926), 441-444.

White, Leonard D. "Scientific Research and State Government," American Political Science Review, XIX (February, 1925), 38-50.

Witte, Edwin E. "Technical Services for State Legislators," Annals, American Academy of Political and Social Science, CVC (January, 1938), 137-143.

Wooddy, Carroll H. "The Legislature: Watch-Dog or House-Dog," State Government, IV (June, 1931), 12-13.

Zeigler, Martha J. "Legislators Work Between Sessions," State Government, X (November, 1937), 236-237.

Selected Unpublished Materials

Moley, Raymond. "The State Movement for Efficiency and Economy." Unpublished Ph.D. Dissertation, Columbia University, New York, 1918.

Smith, David W. "The Legislative Council Movement in the United States." Unpublished Ph.D. dissertation, Department of Political Science, University of Utah, 1955.

Smith, T. V. "The Biography of a Bill." The text of an address to the Legislative Service Conference, New Orleans, Louisiana, September 28, 1953.

INDEX

Elliott, William Yandell, 231

Ely, Richard T., 25

"Fact-finding" and the legislative process, 35-36, 218 ff.

Federalism, 228 ff.

Florida Legislative Council, 110, 123

Florida Legislative Research Bureau, 34, 41

Florida Statute Revision and Bill Drafting Departments, 33, 41

Freund, Ernst, 30

Frontier, political significance, 9-10; and Wisconsin, 24-25

Gaus, John M., ix; quoted, 55

Georgia Bill Drafting Unit, 34, 41

Georgia State Library, 41

Godkin, E. L., 12-13

Gove, Samuel K., x

Governor, as legislative leader, 15-16, 202-203; in New York, 24; and legislature in 1919 Model State Constitution proposals, 48

Governor, relations with legislative council, 69, 112; in Illinois, 149 ff., 156-157; in Kansas, 93 ff.; in Kentucky, 164-165, 170, 175 ff., in Minnesota, 204; in Nebraska, 195; in Wisconsin, 187, 189-190

Graves, W. Brooke, x, 60 n.

Guild, Frederick H., ix, 64, 115, 164; creation of Kansas Legislative Council, 66 ff.; spread of councils and council-type agencies, 67-68

Hatton, A. R., 62, 64

Holcombe, Arthur W., 47, 113

Illinois Legislative Council, 33, 41, 110, 112, 126, 129 ff.; and governor, 149, 152; and interim committees, 146-147; and legislative reference bureau, 148,

260   The Legislative Council in the American States

Legislative procedure; development of, 7, 10 ff.; inadequacies, 23; in Illinois, 150-151; in Kansas, 80, 91;
in Kentucky, 179-180

Legislative Reference Bureau, U.S. Congress, 29-30

Legislative reference bureaus; atrophy, 222; establishment, 33-34 (table), 41-45 (table); functions, 41-45
(table); fundamental concepts, 25, 30, 31, 35-36

Legislative reference and research services (see also
legislative councils and "council type agencies");
as substitutes for legislative councils, 220-221;
evaluated, 30-31, 32-33, 35; separate from legislatures, 35, 212; early spread, 27 ff.; second phase in
the spread of, 32, 33-34 (table), 119, 212; the literature, 27, 38-39 n.

Legislative reform; and American Legislators' Association, 52 ff.; and 20th Century reorganization movement, 16; future prospects for, 227-228; need for,
in 1930's, 56-58; needs and developments, 1933-
1958, 118-119, 227

Legislative Research Checklist, 122 n.

Legislative Service Conference, 116-117, 169, 201

Legislative span of control, problem of, 219, 223

Legislative staff services, modern development, 211 ff.;
proposed integration of, 201

Legislative supremacy, 7-9; and legislative councils,
119

Legislative voting machines, 56, 60 n.

Legislator; the amateur citizen legislator, 10, 51, 56,
57, 145, 201 ff.; his need for technical knowledge,
221 ff.; role in the Kansas council, 87 ff.; in Illinois,
145, 150-151

Legislature, theory of; amateur citizen-legislator, 10,
51, 56, 57, 201 ff., 223; and legislative reference
work, 35-36; colonial theory, 5 ff.; diversity among
state legislatures, 211, 216, 224; legislature as
process, 216 ff., 226; legislature and policy-making,
224 ff.; legislature and leadership, 218-219; John
Stuart Mill, 25-26, 50-51

Representation, geographical, development of, 6

Representation, property as a basis for, 6

Rhode Island Assistant in Charge of Law Revision, 44

Rhode Island Legislative Council, 112

Rhode Island Legislative Reference Bureau, 44

Rodgers, Jack W., ix

Sachse, Earl, ix

Senning, John P., x, 112-113, 196

Separation of powers; and 1919 and 1920 Model Constitution proposals, 48-50; in Kansas, 93; as basis for
legislative council, 156; and legislative oversight of
administration, 201-202

Short, Lloyd M., x

Skipton, John A., ix

Smith, T. V., x, 112, 129 ff., 158 n., 159 n.

South Carolina Legislative Council, 110, 127, 192

South Dakota Legislative Research Council, 111, 124,
192, 193

South Dakota Revisor of Statutes, 34, 44

Spelman Fund, 53, 54, 66-67

State government; expenditures, 231; "financial middlemen," 232; recent growth, 231, 232; reorganization,
16

State libraries, 23, 35, 41 ff.

State manager plan proposal, 47 ff.

State reorganization studies; Illinois Shaefer Commission, 147; Kansas, 96; Kentucky, 166

State statutes, growth in volume, 20 n., 22

States and national centralization, 9-10, 60-61 n., 119,
228 ff., 232

Steiner, Gilbert Y., x

Strain, Camden, 62, 66, 69